I0698360

To every young artist,

May your colors be as bold as your dreams. This book is for you, the magical hands that bring these pages to life. Happy coloring!

— Tainá Oishi"

Tainá Oishi 2024

This Book Belongs to:

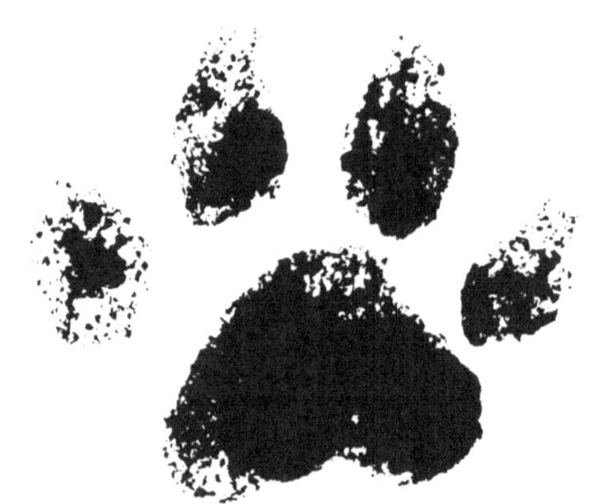

Test Color Page

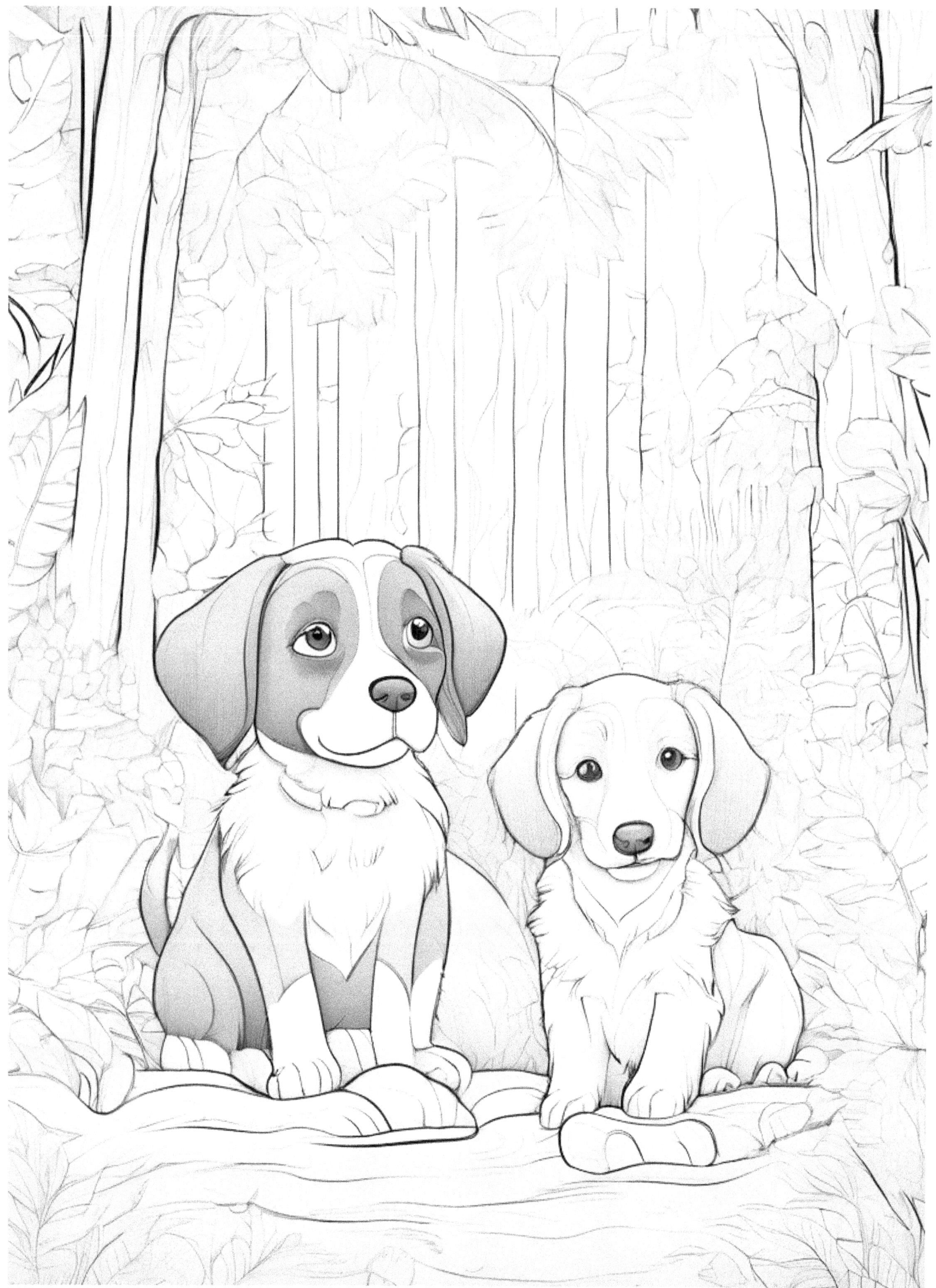

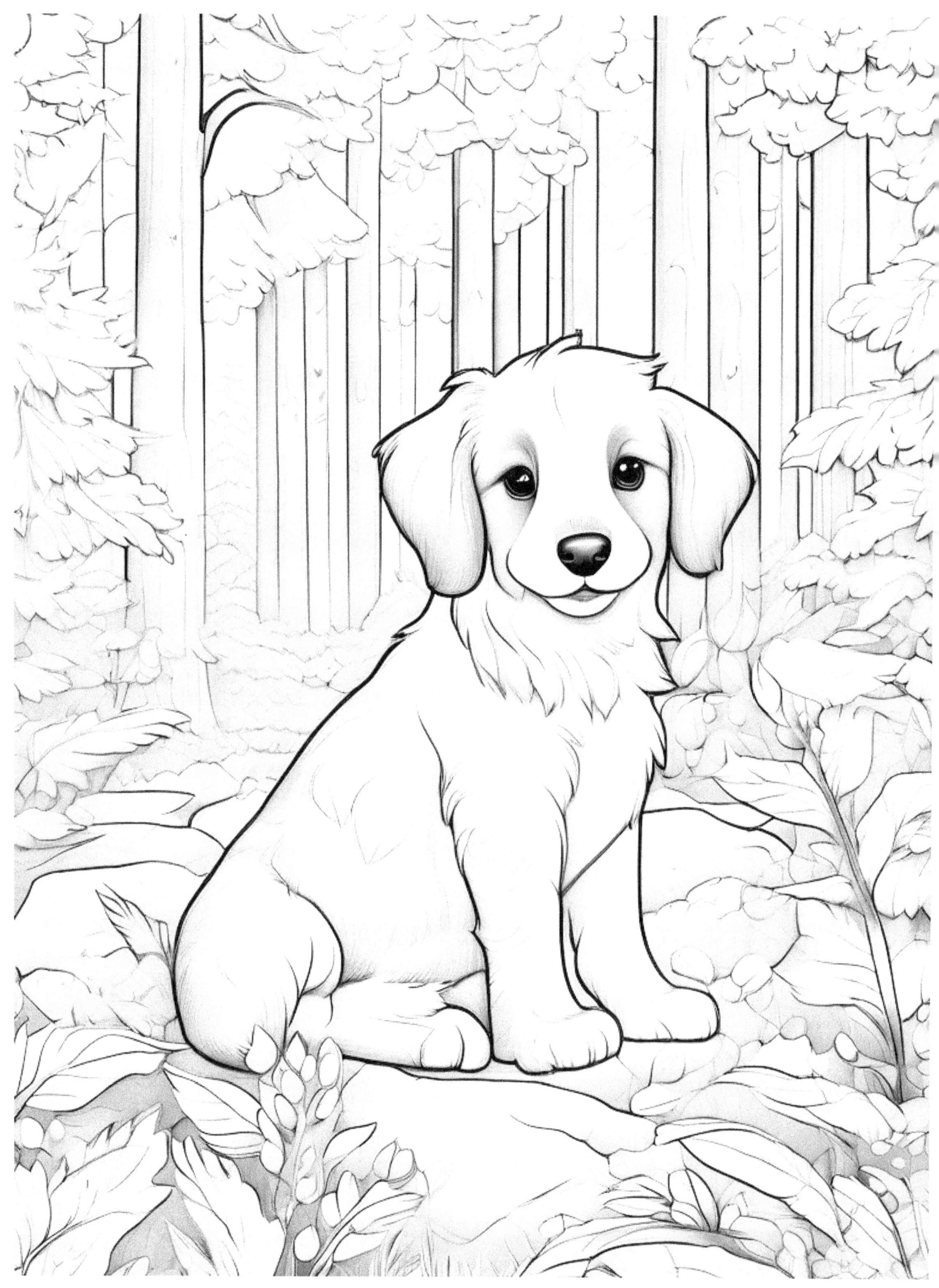

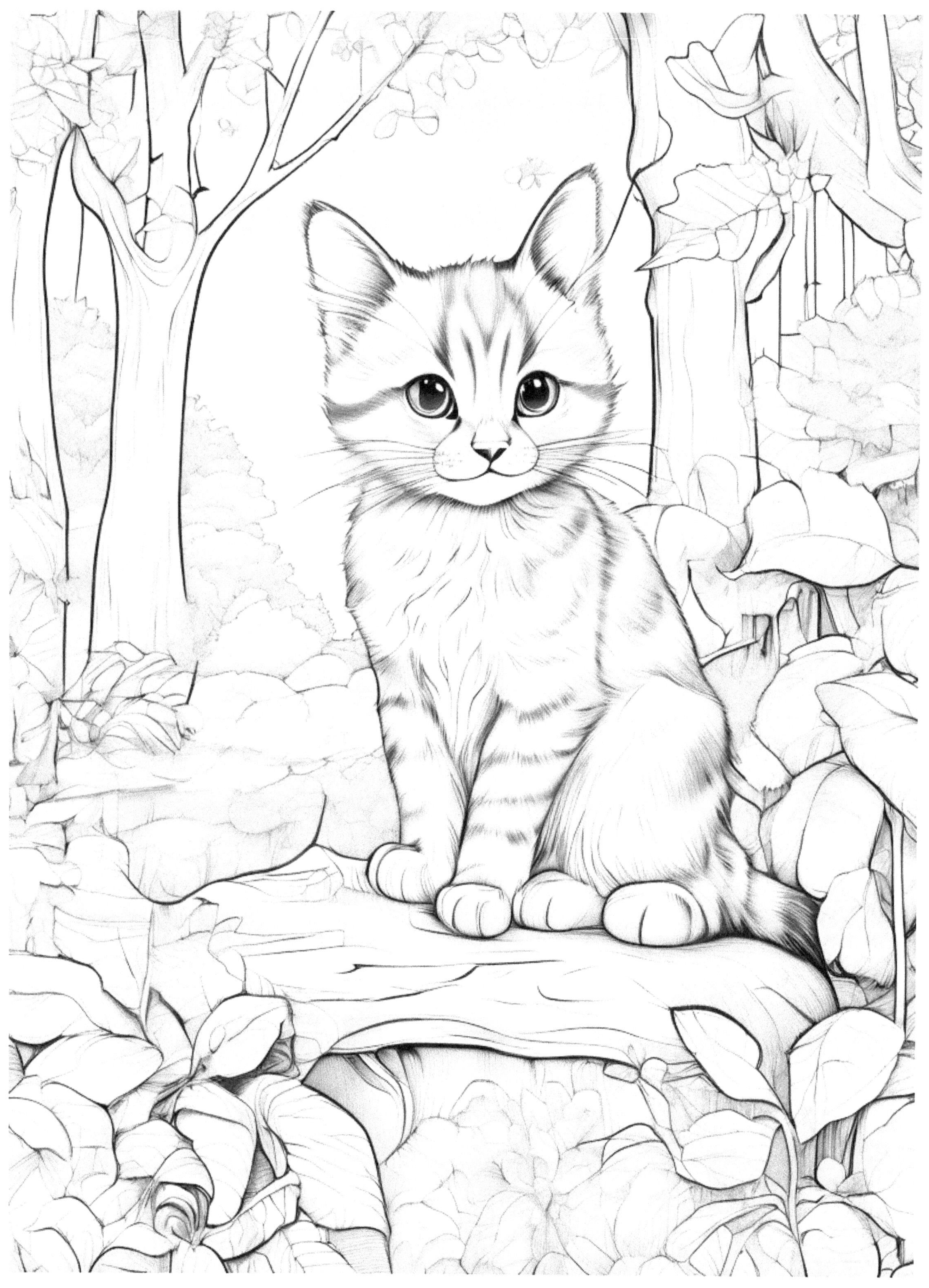

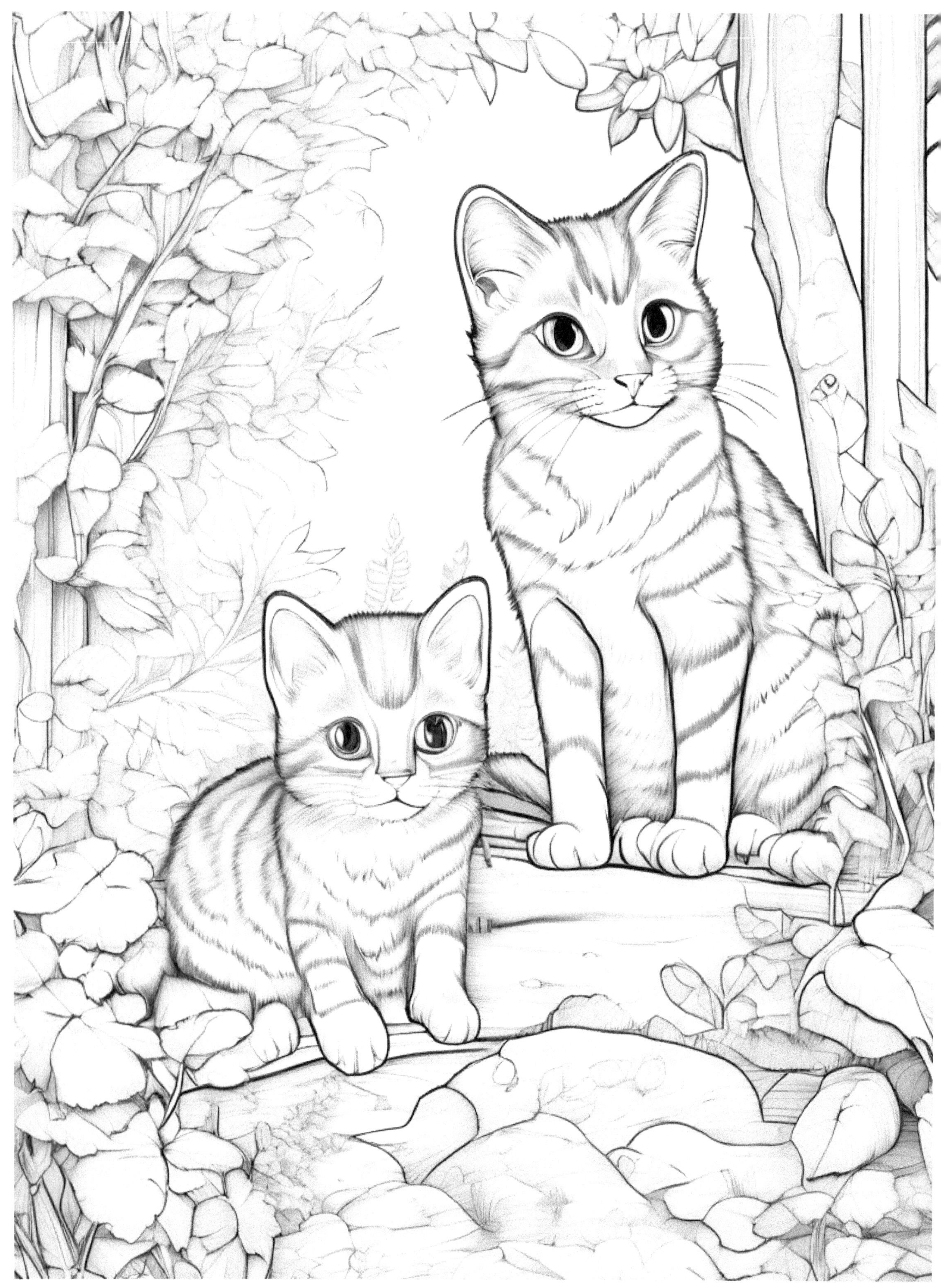

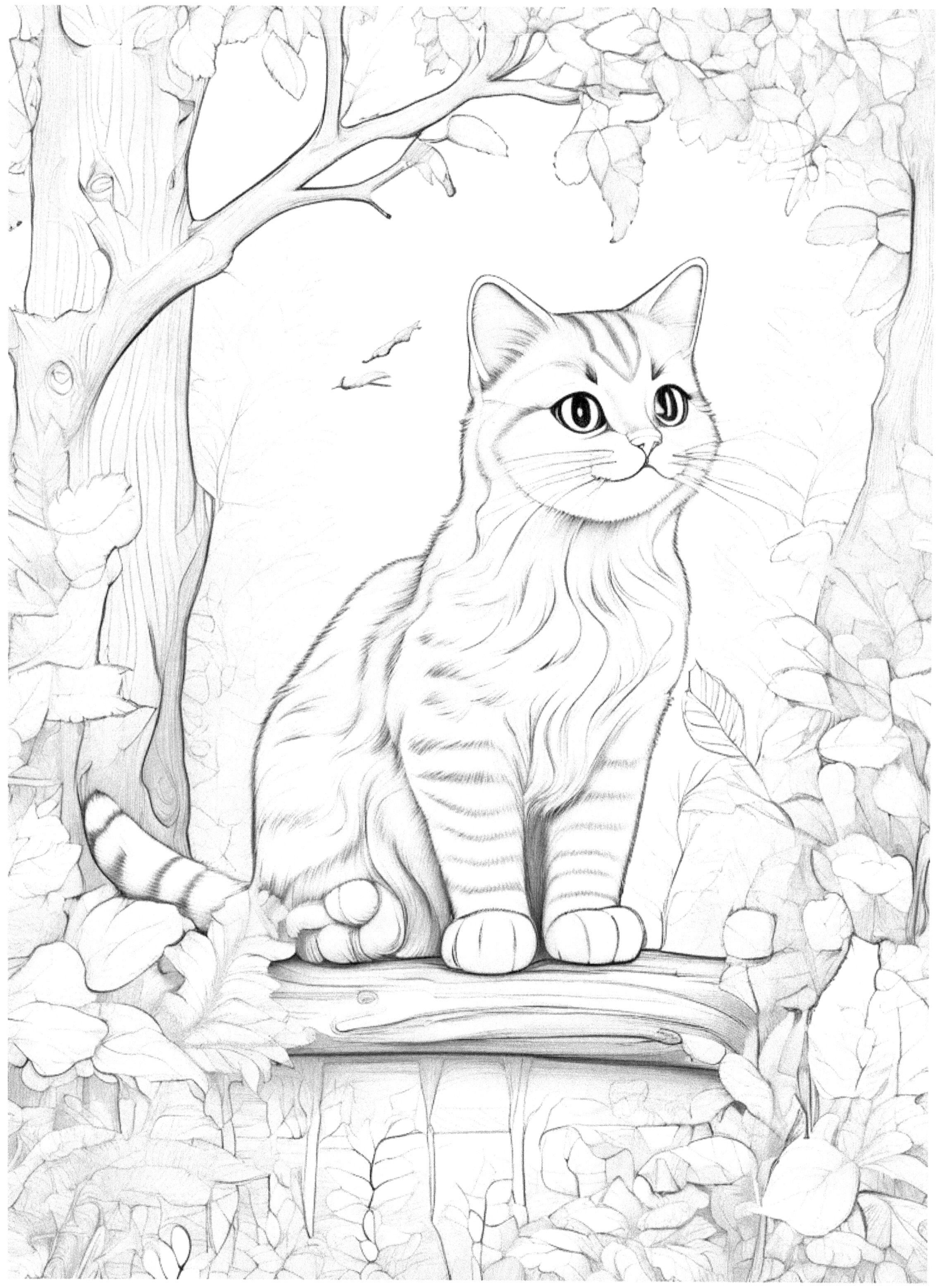

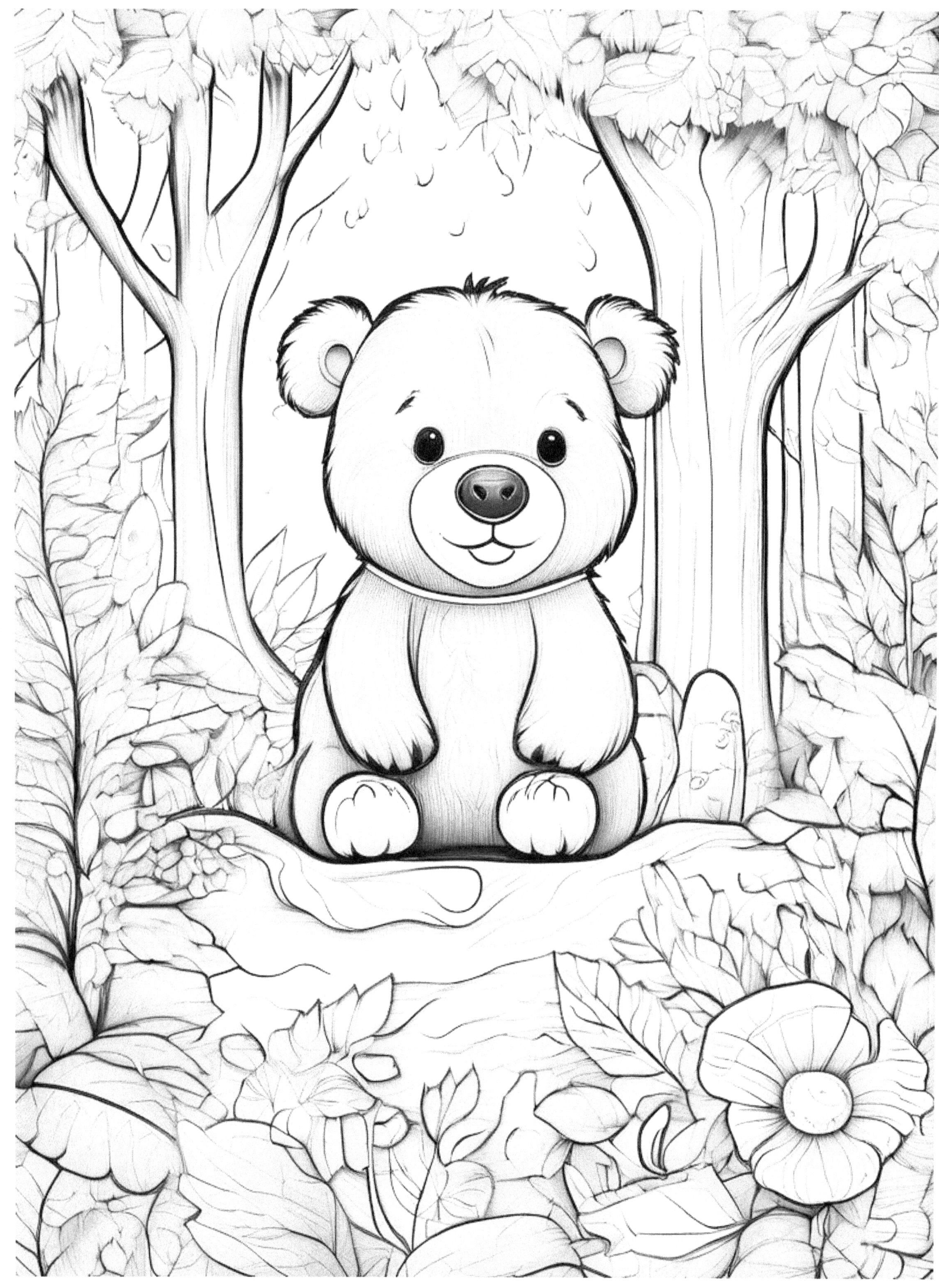

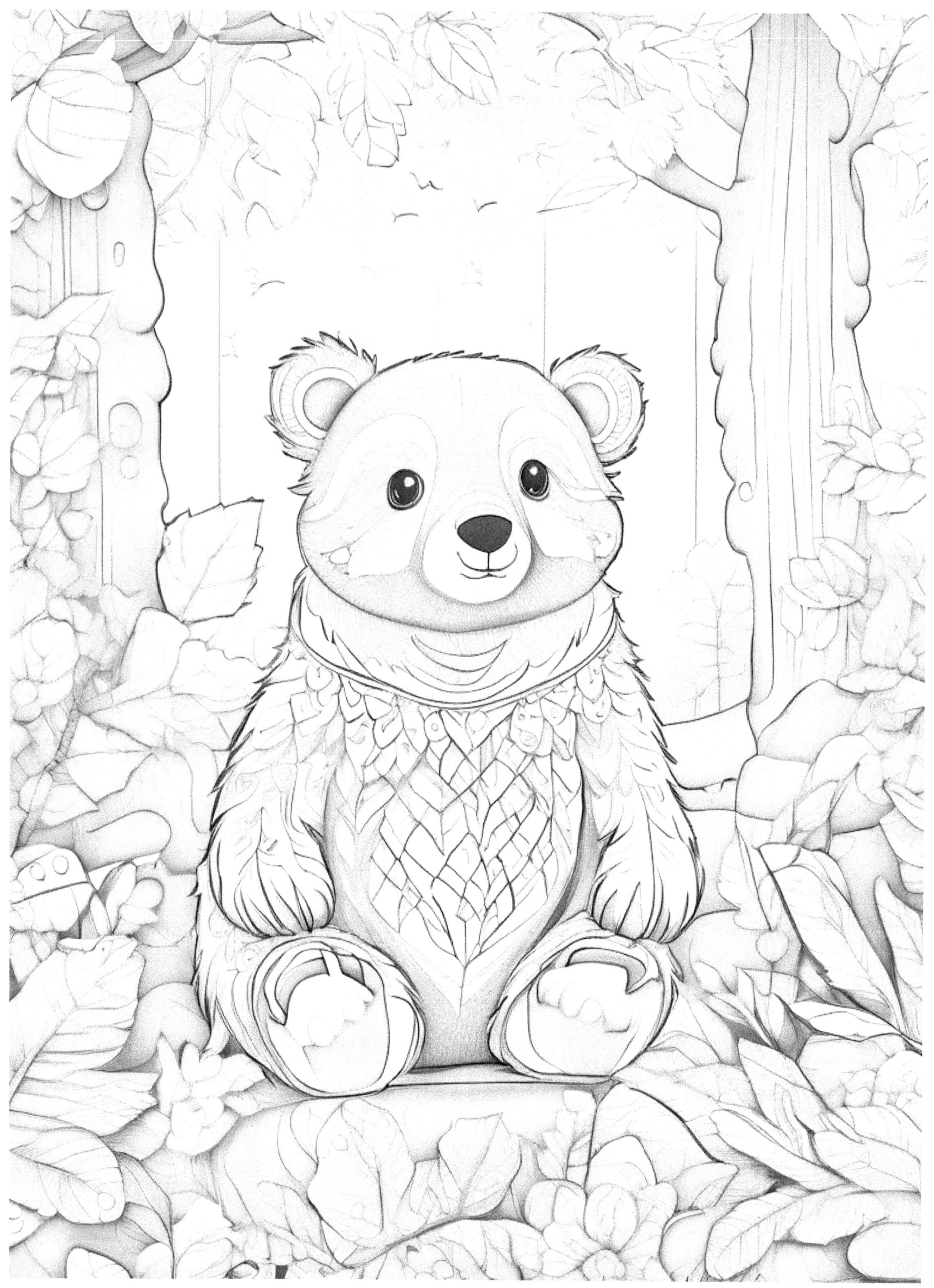

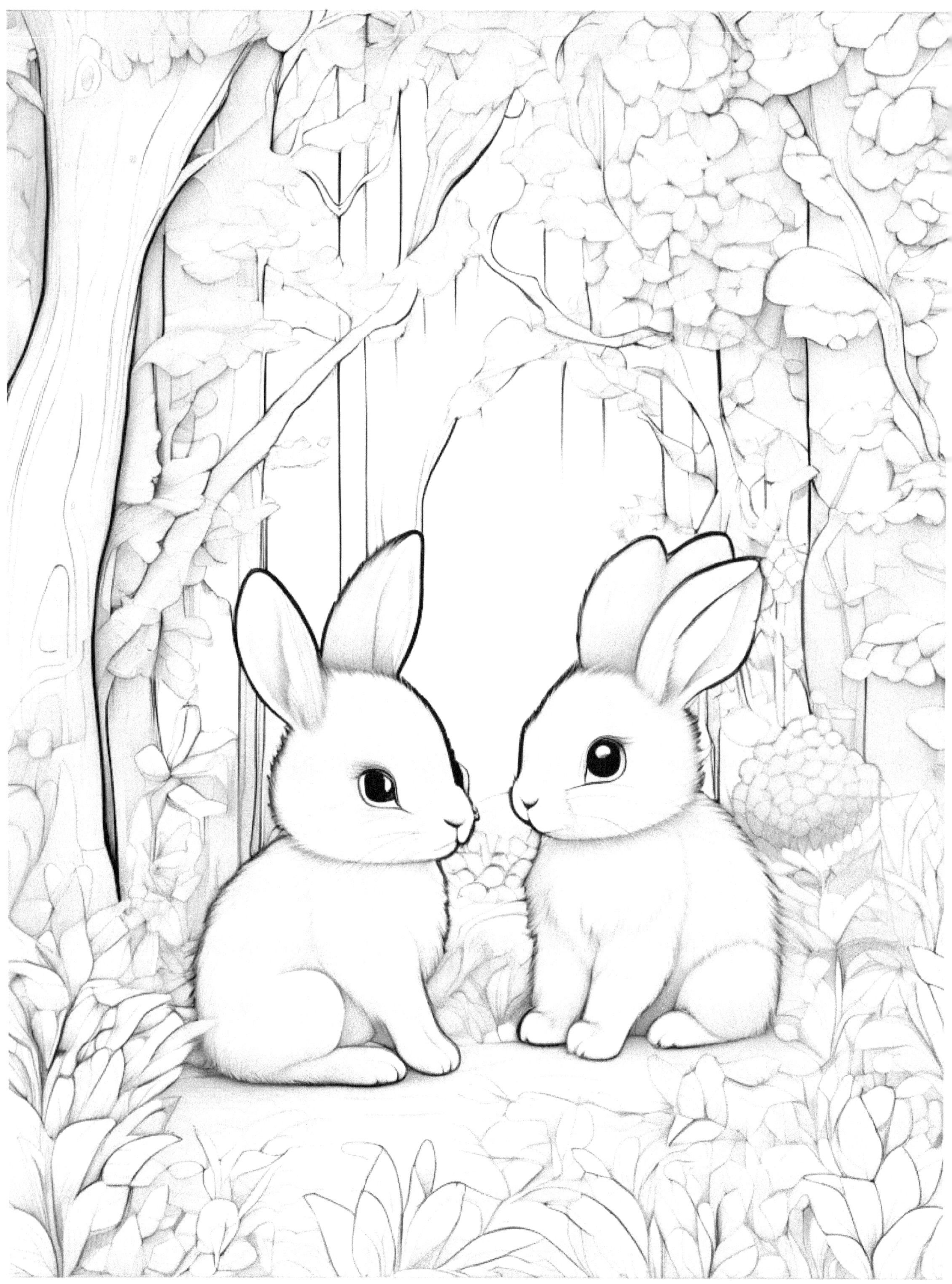

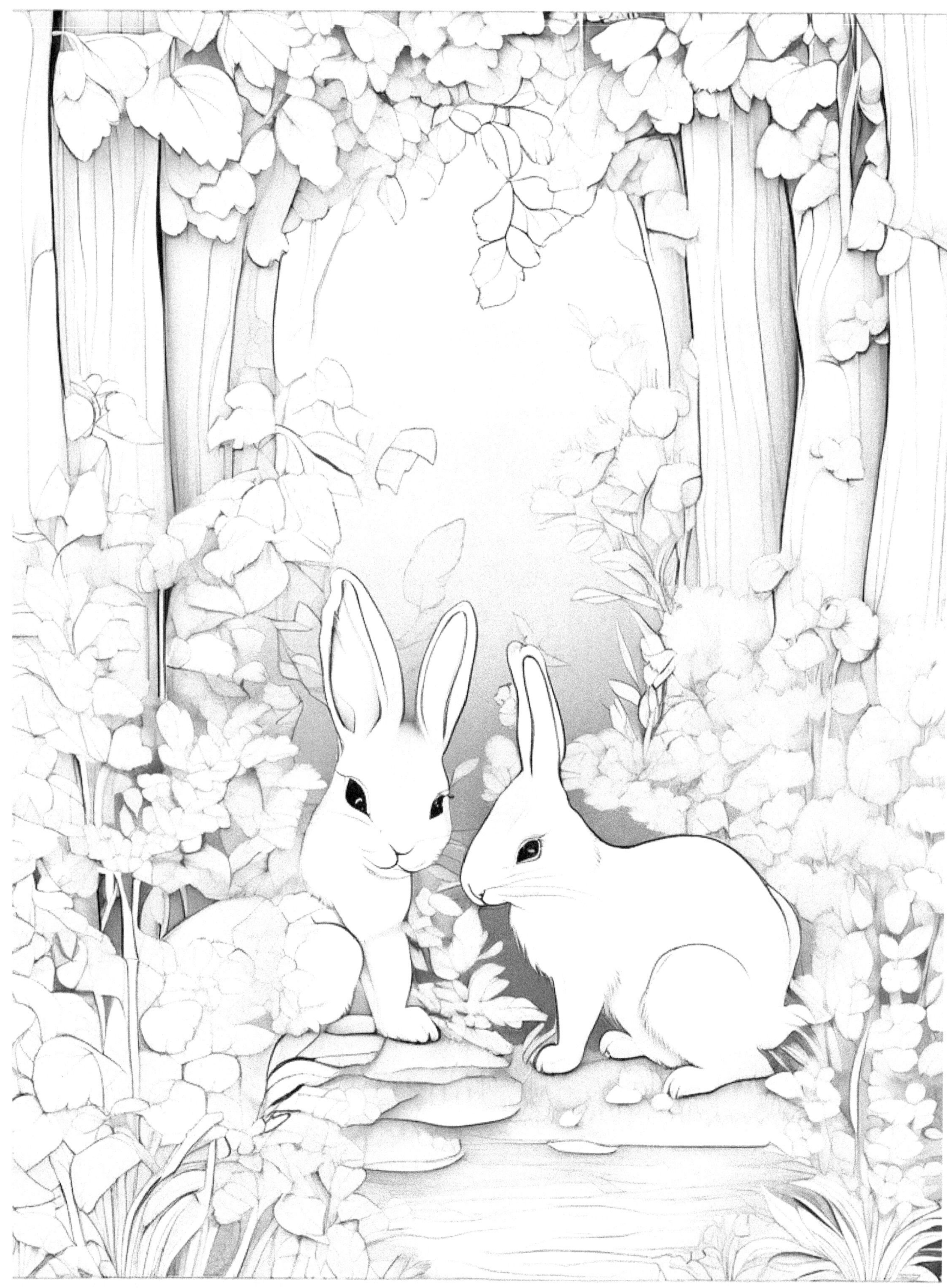

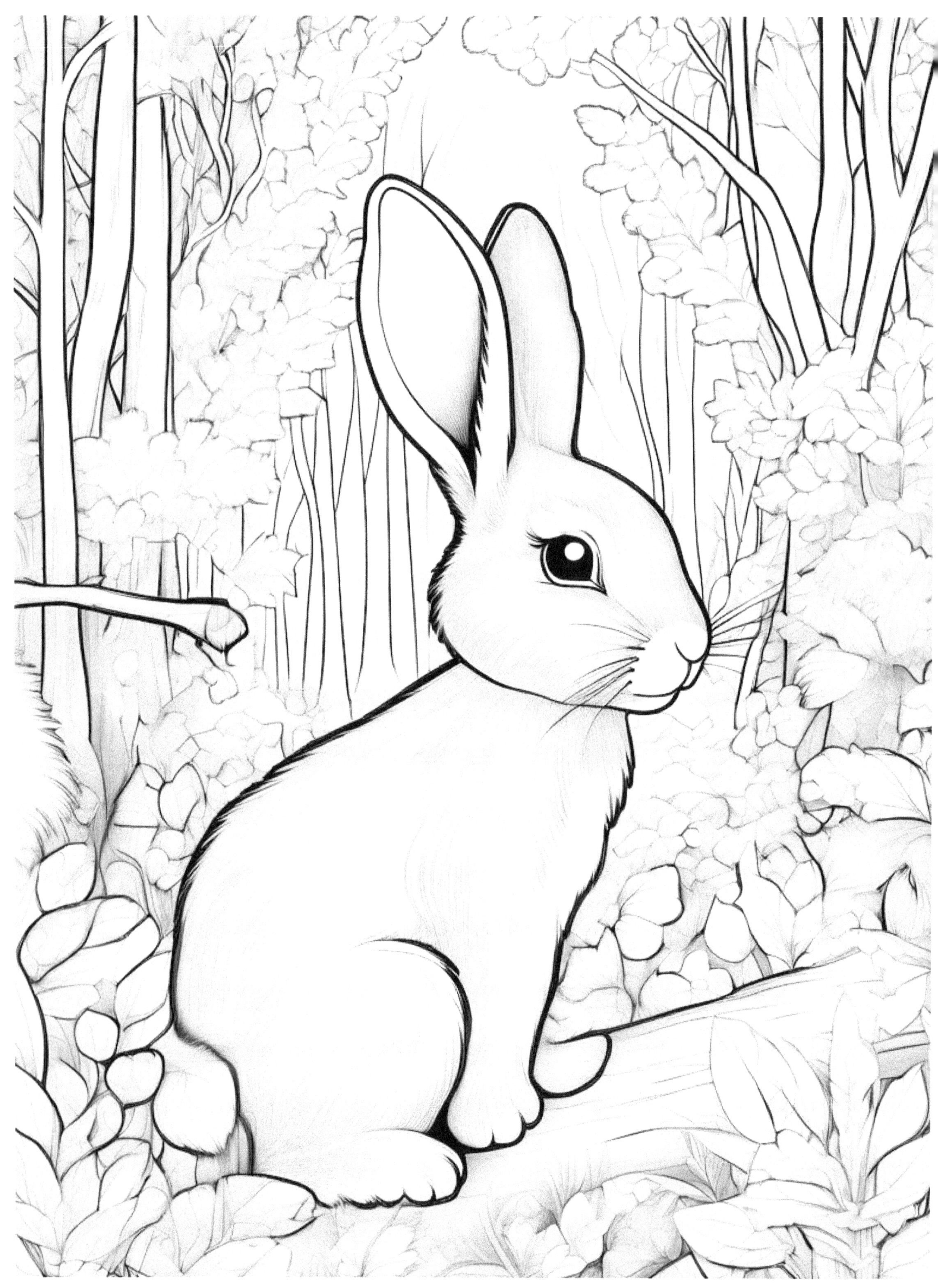

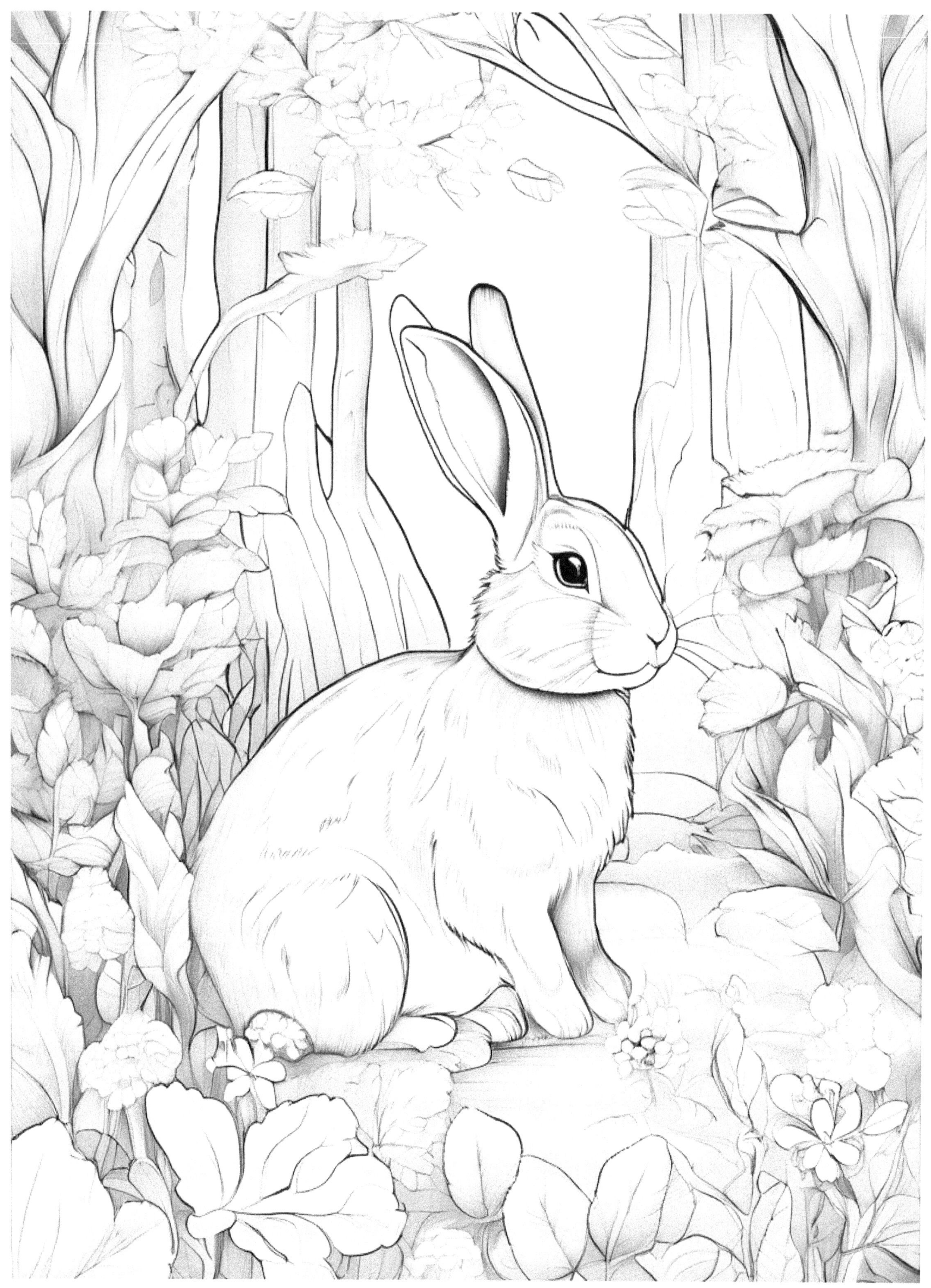

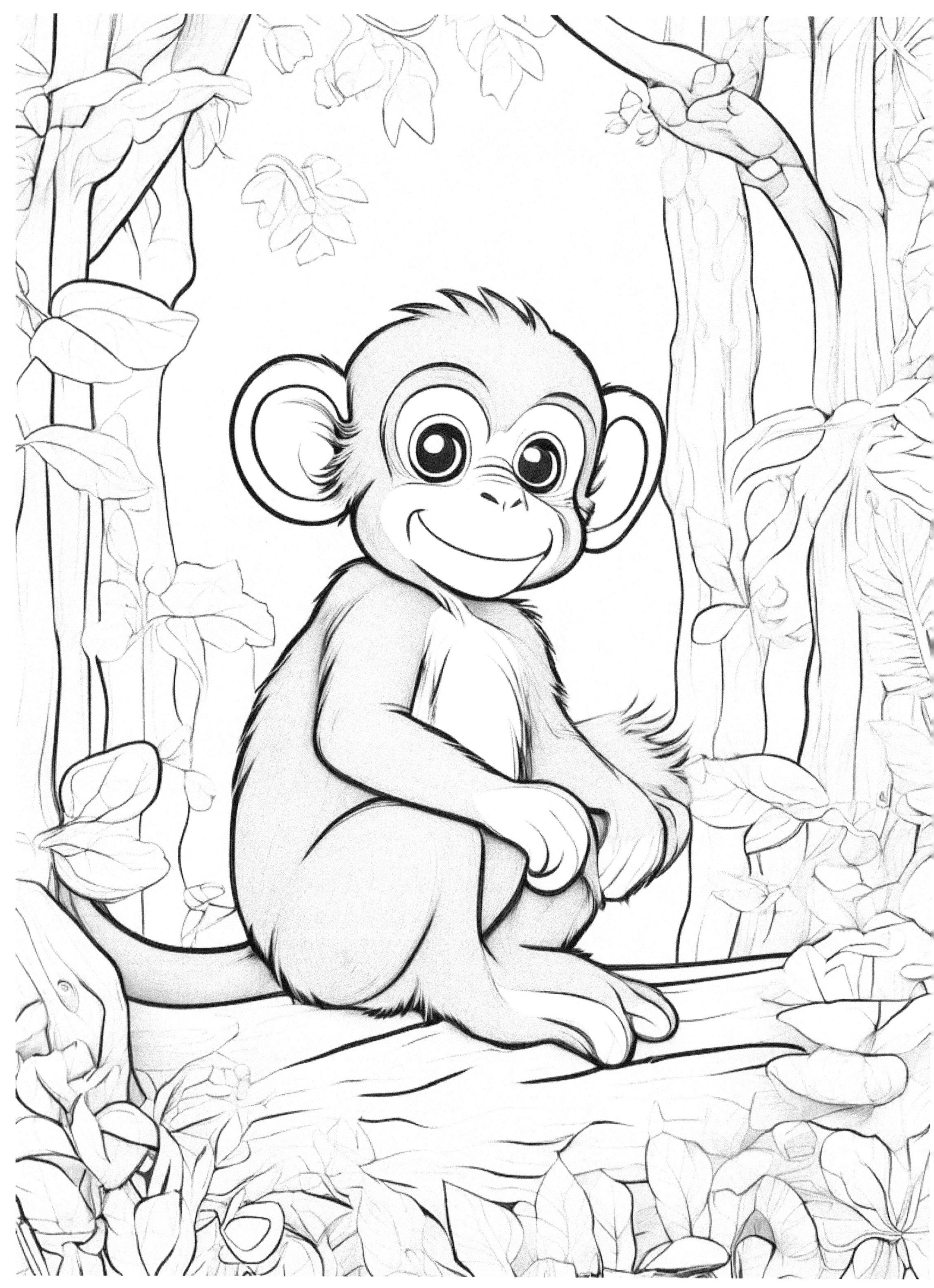

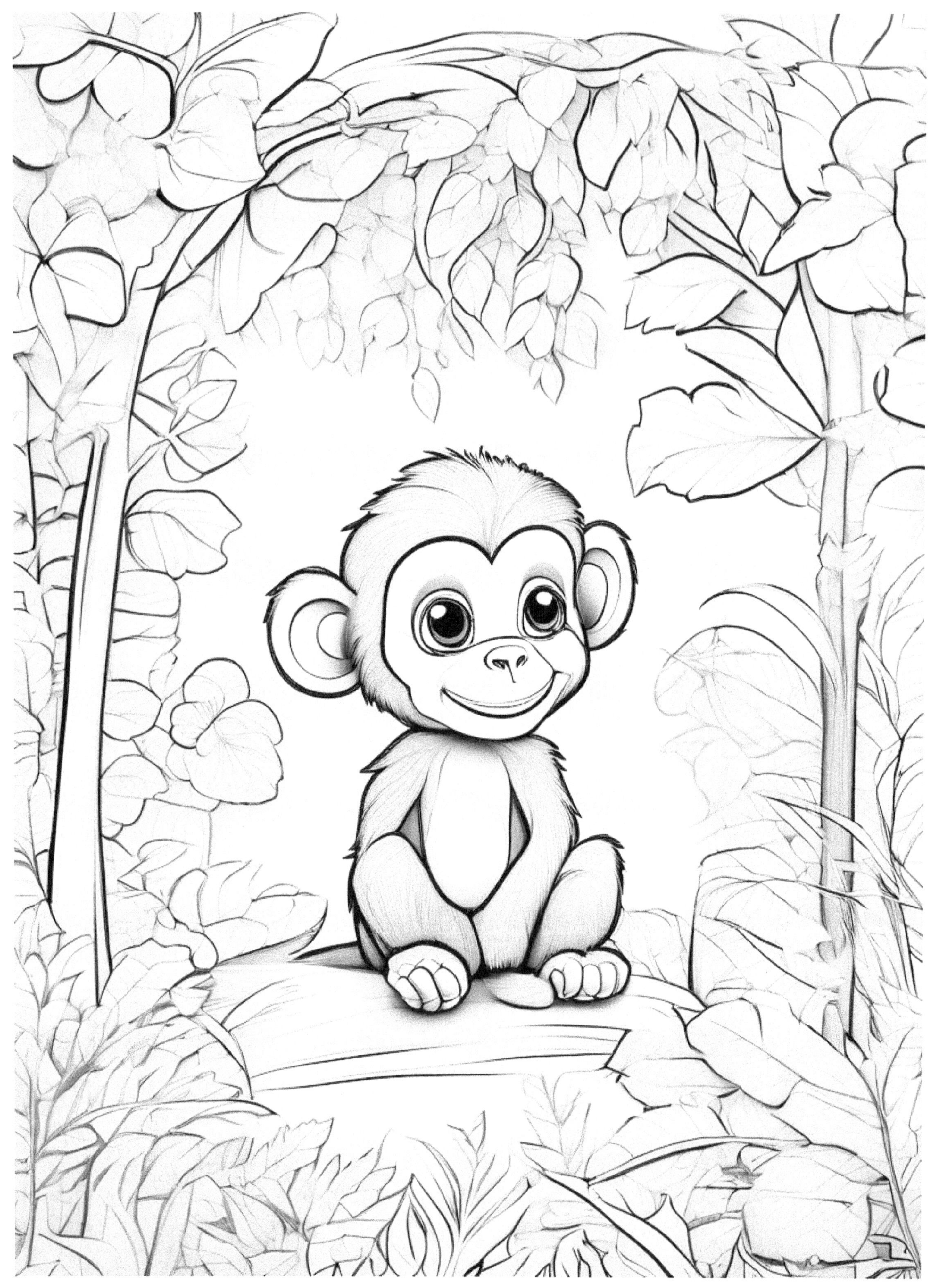

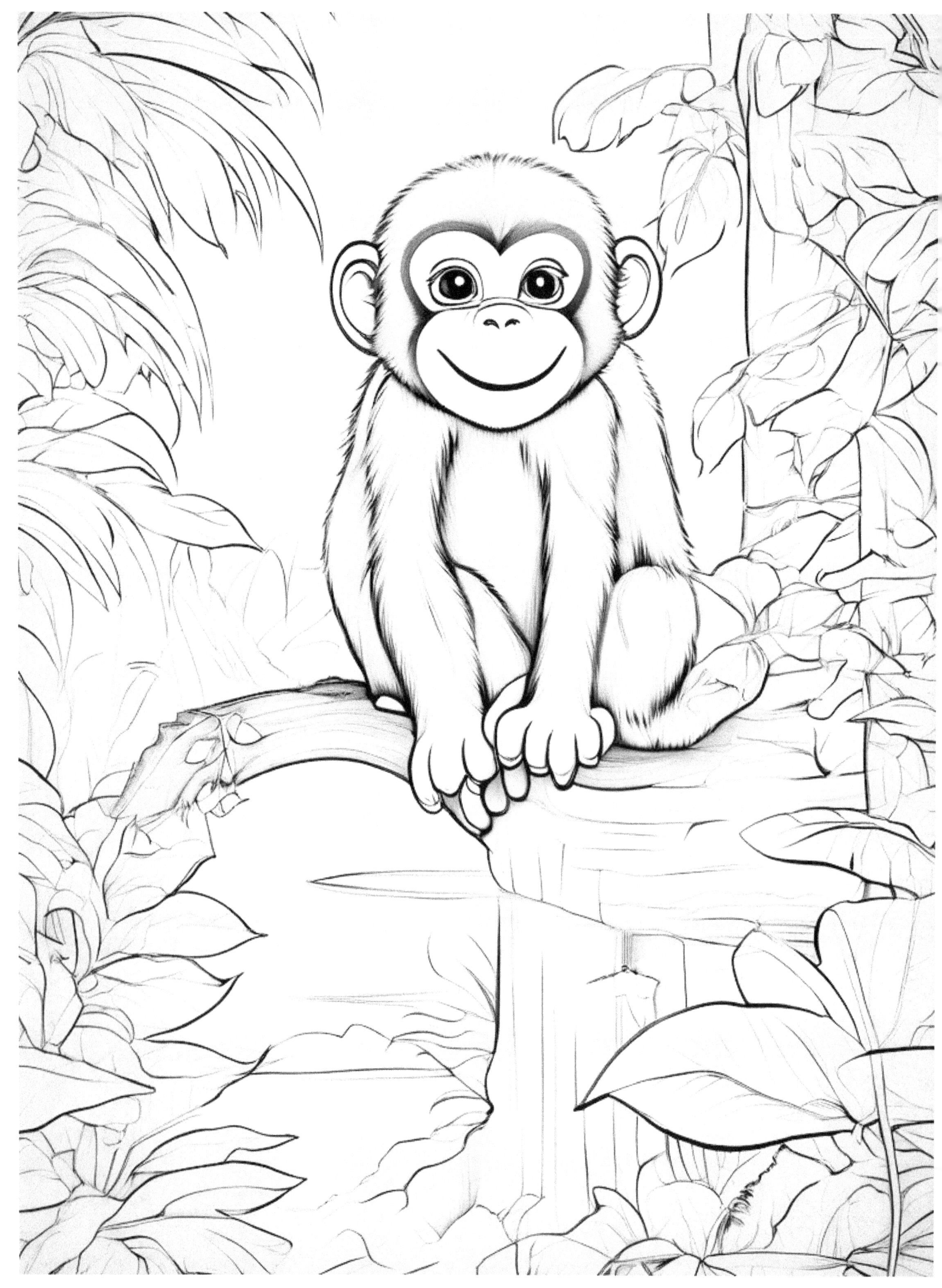

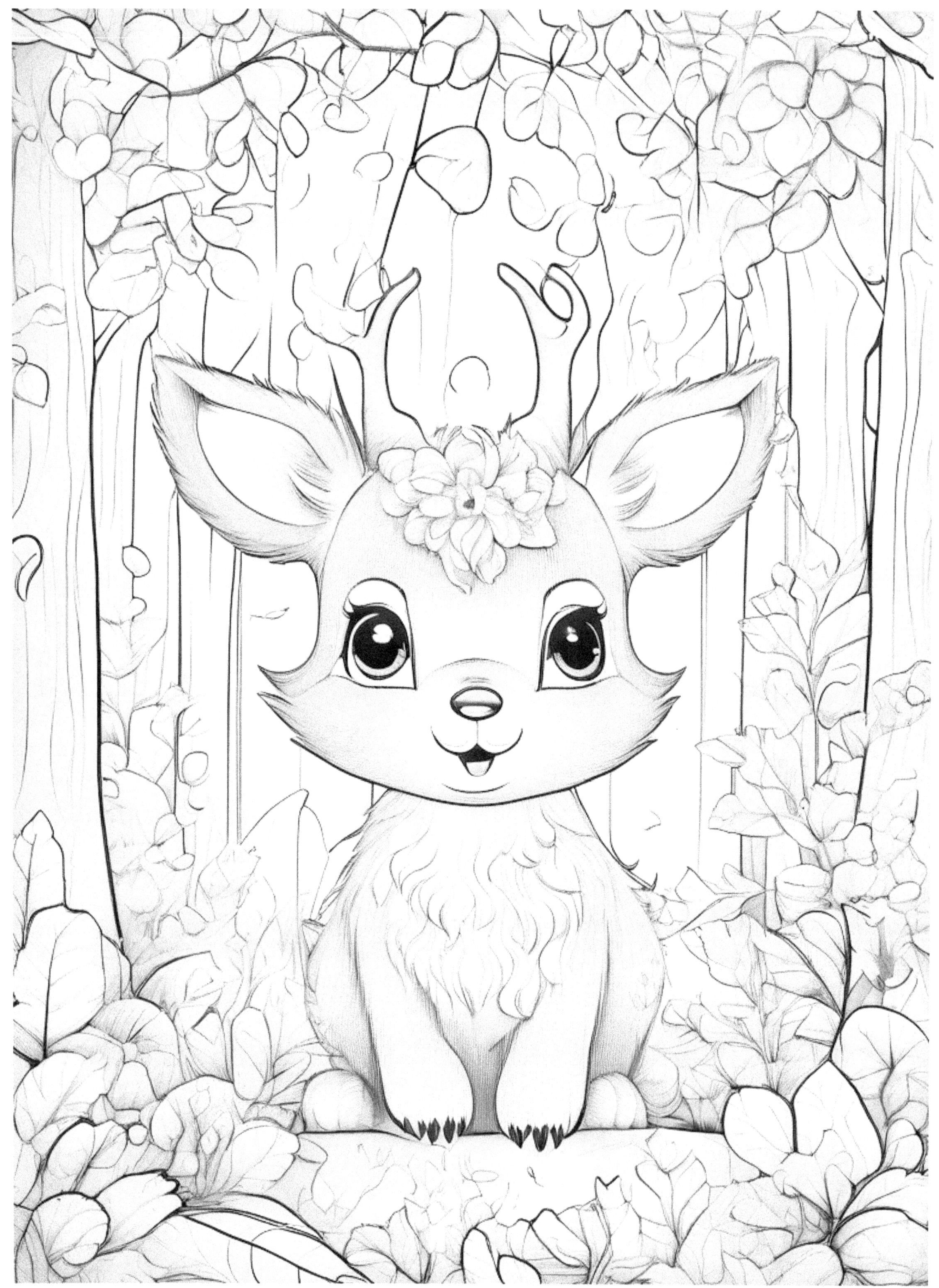

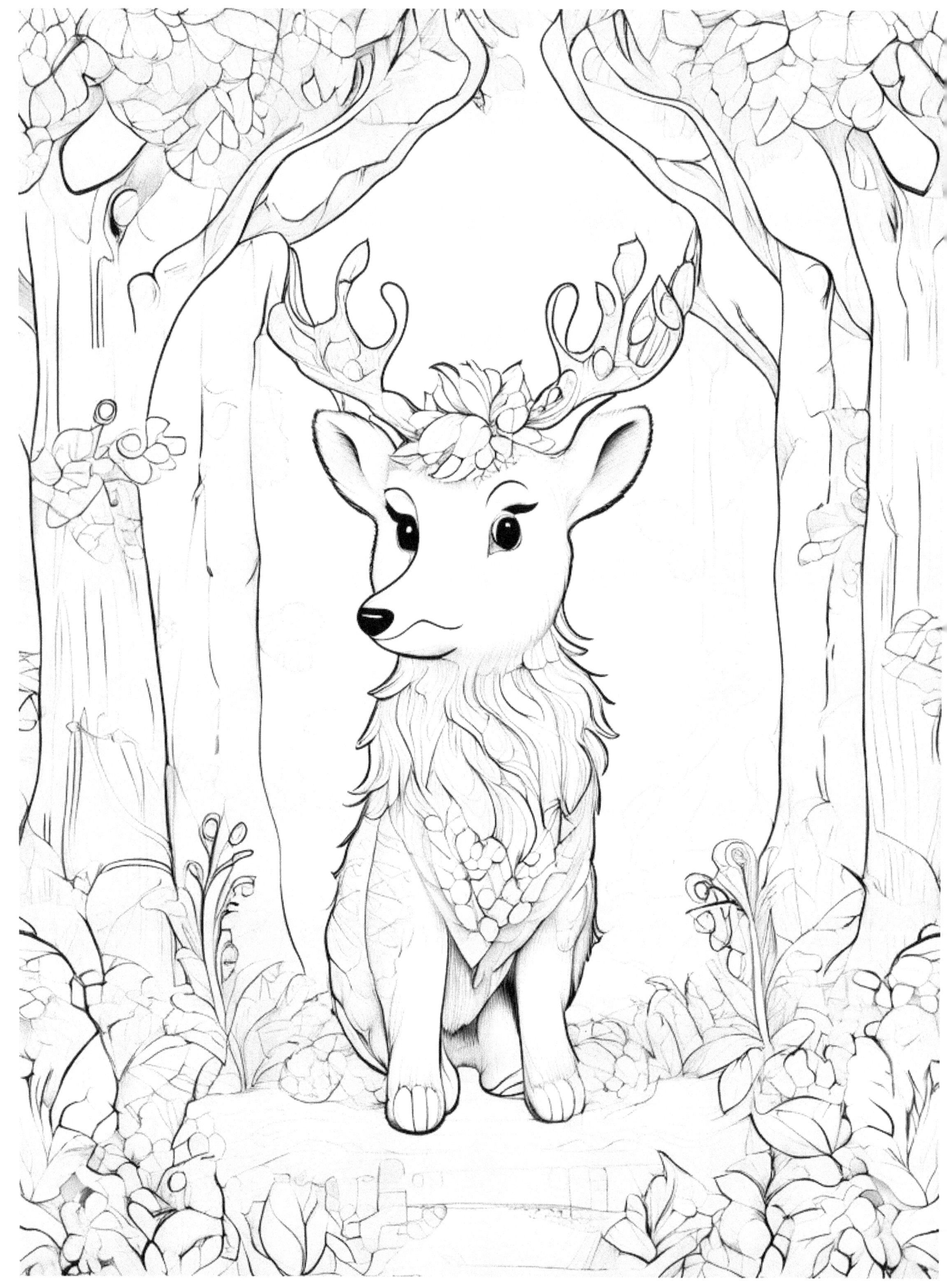

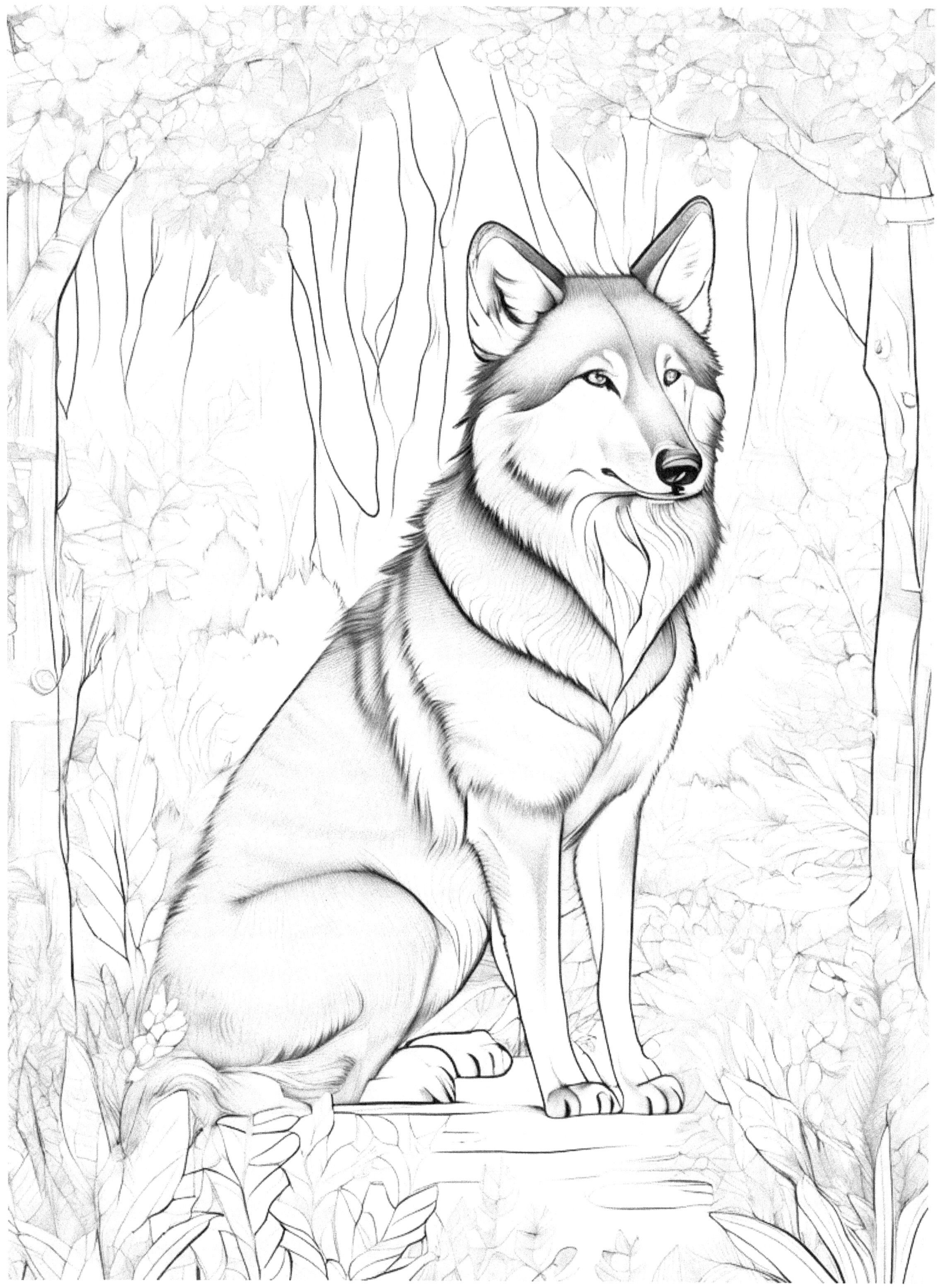

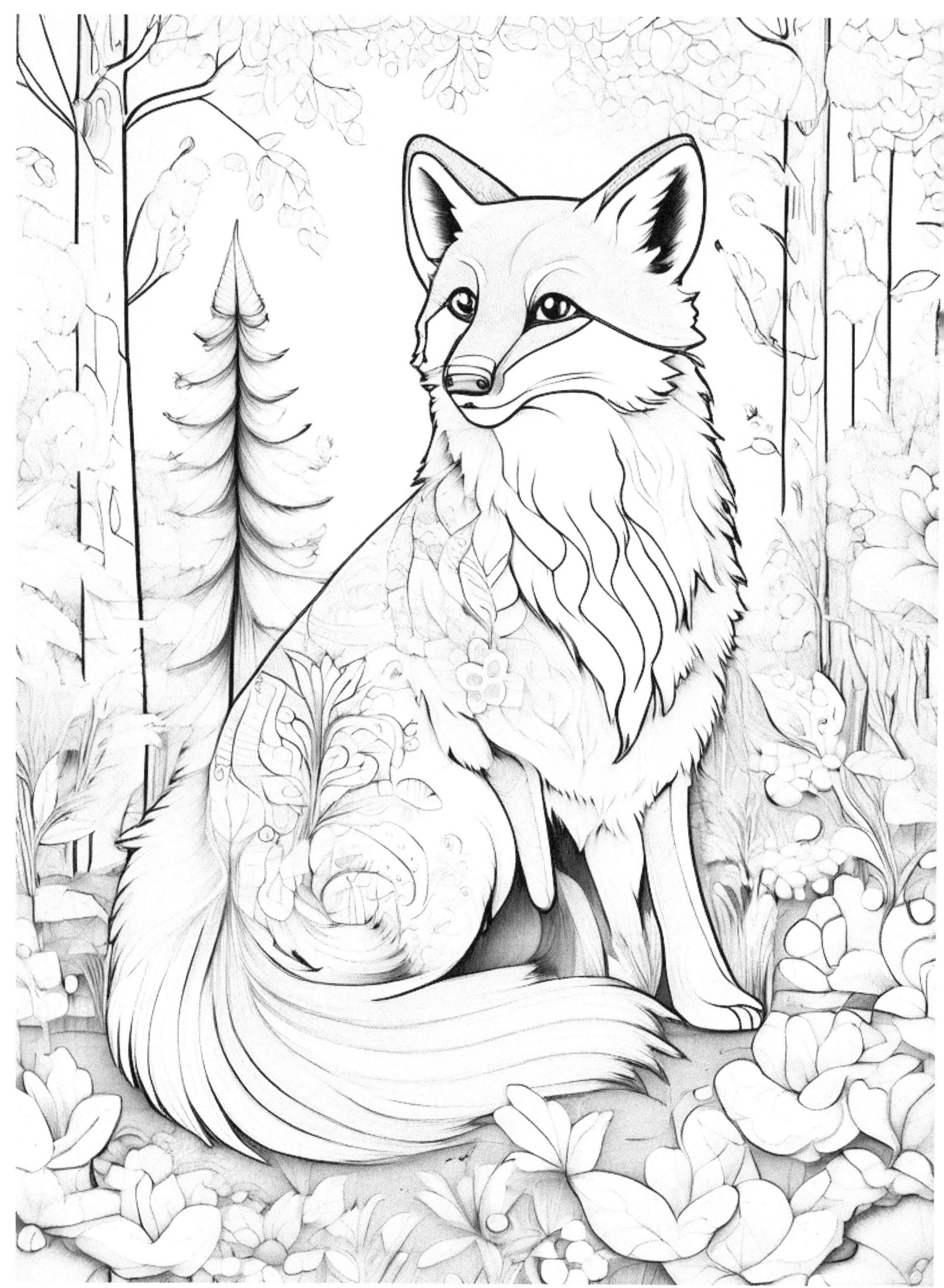

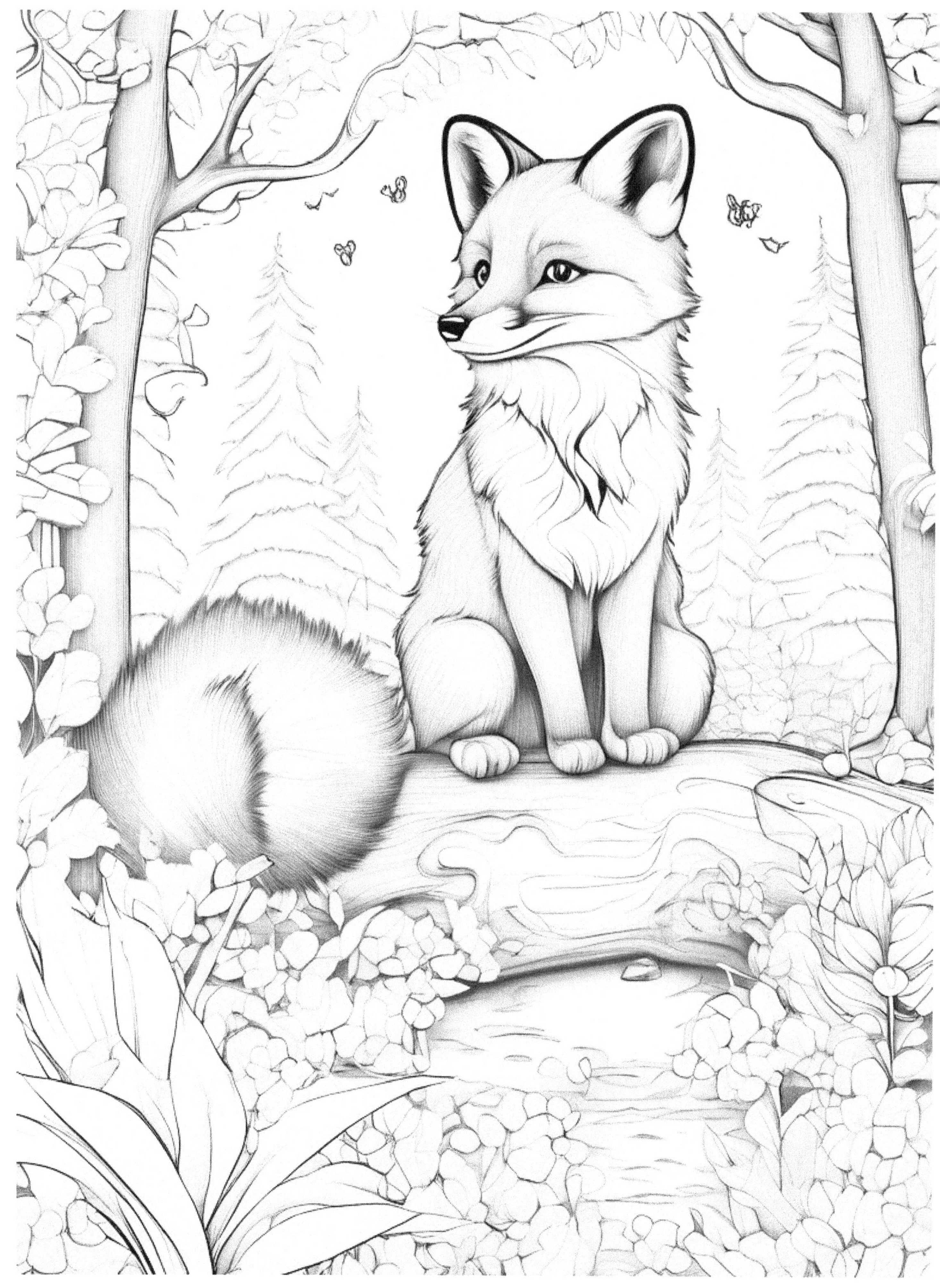

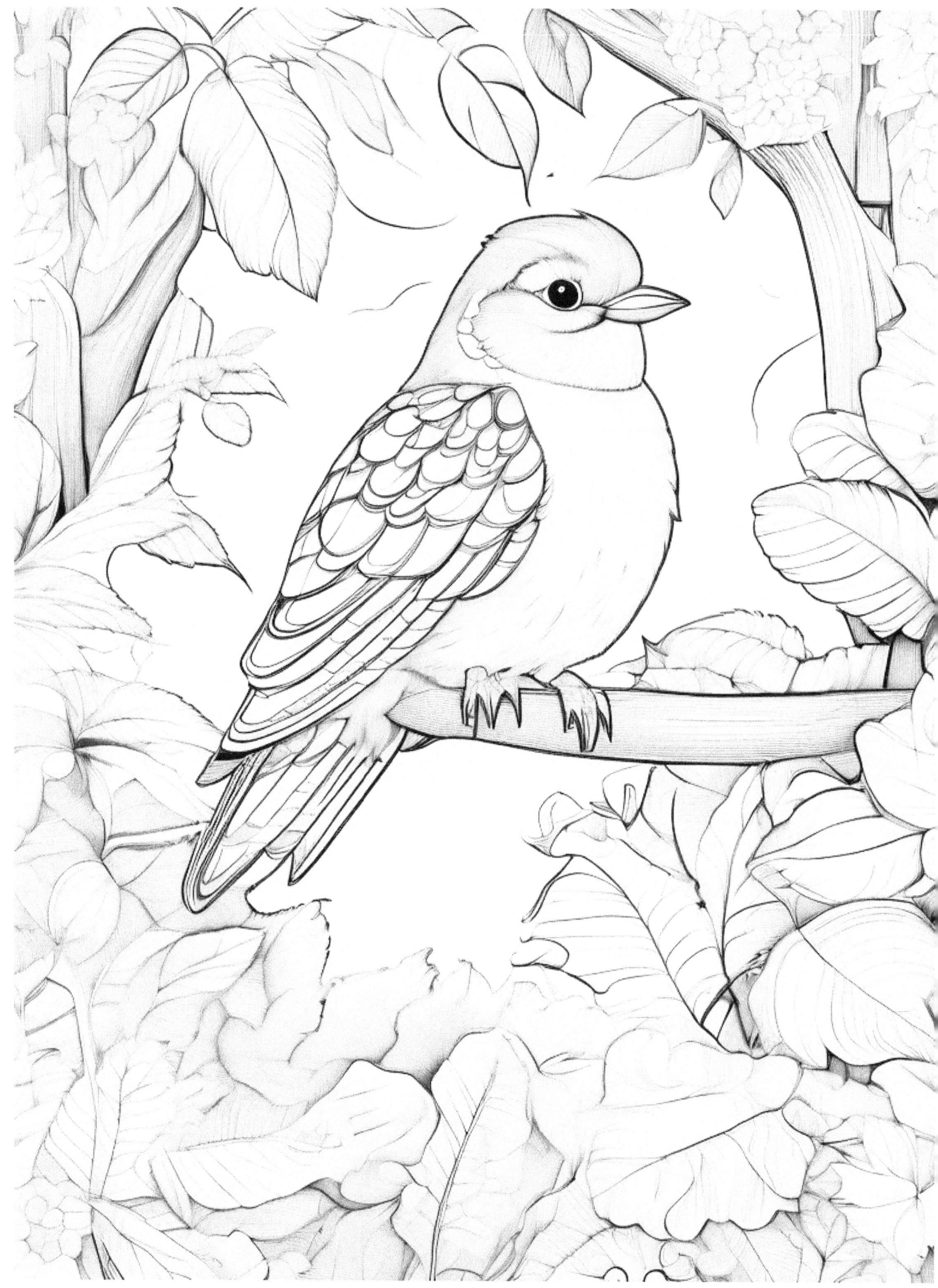

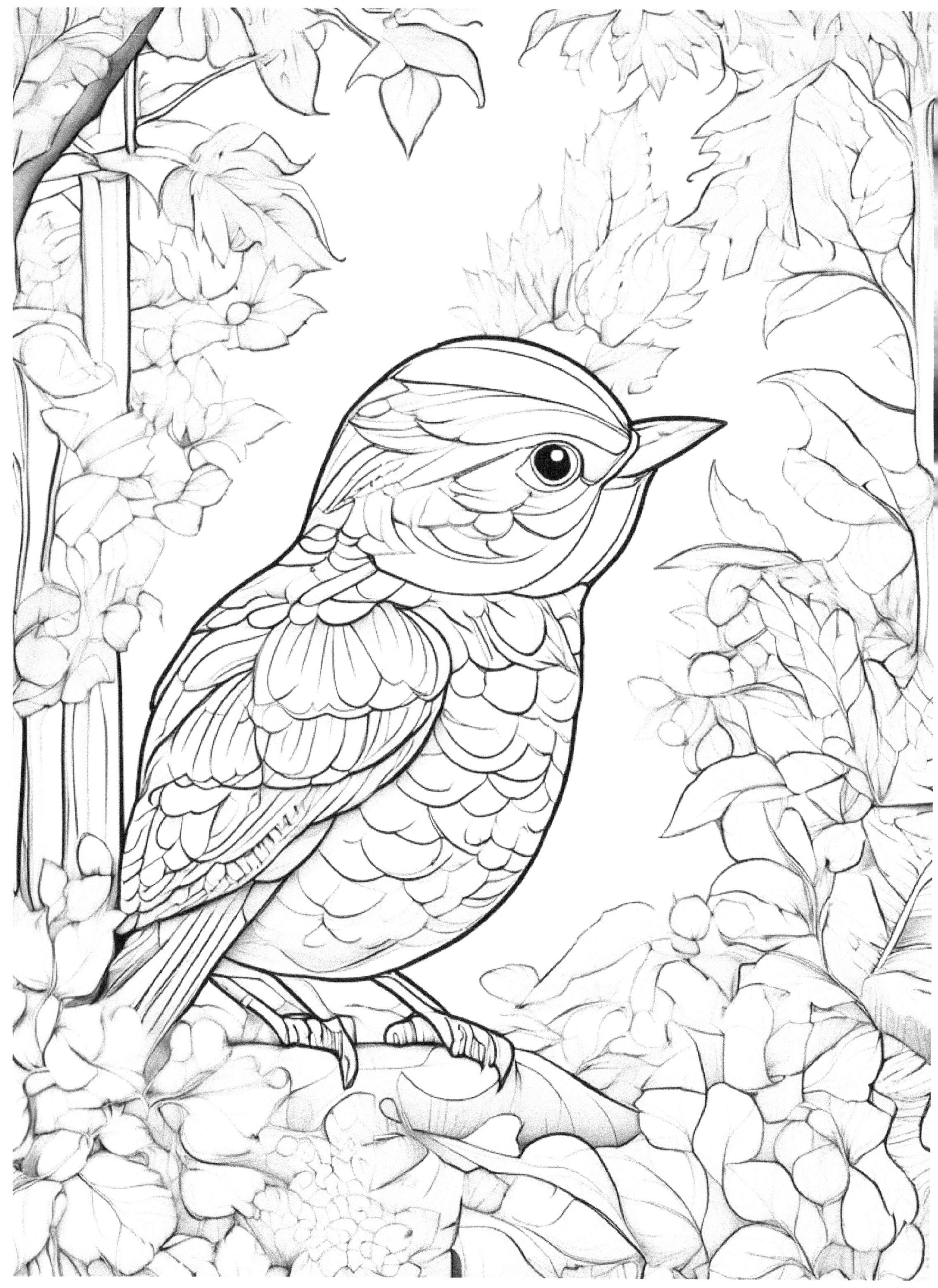

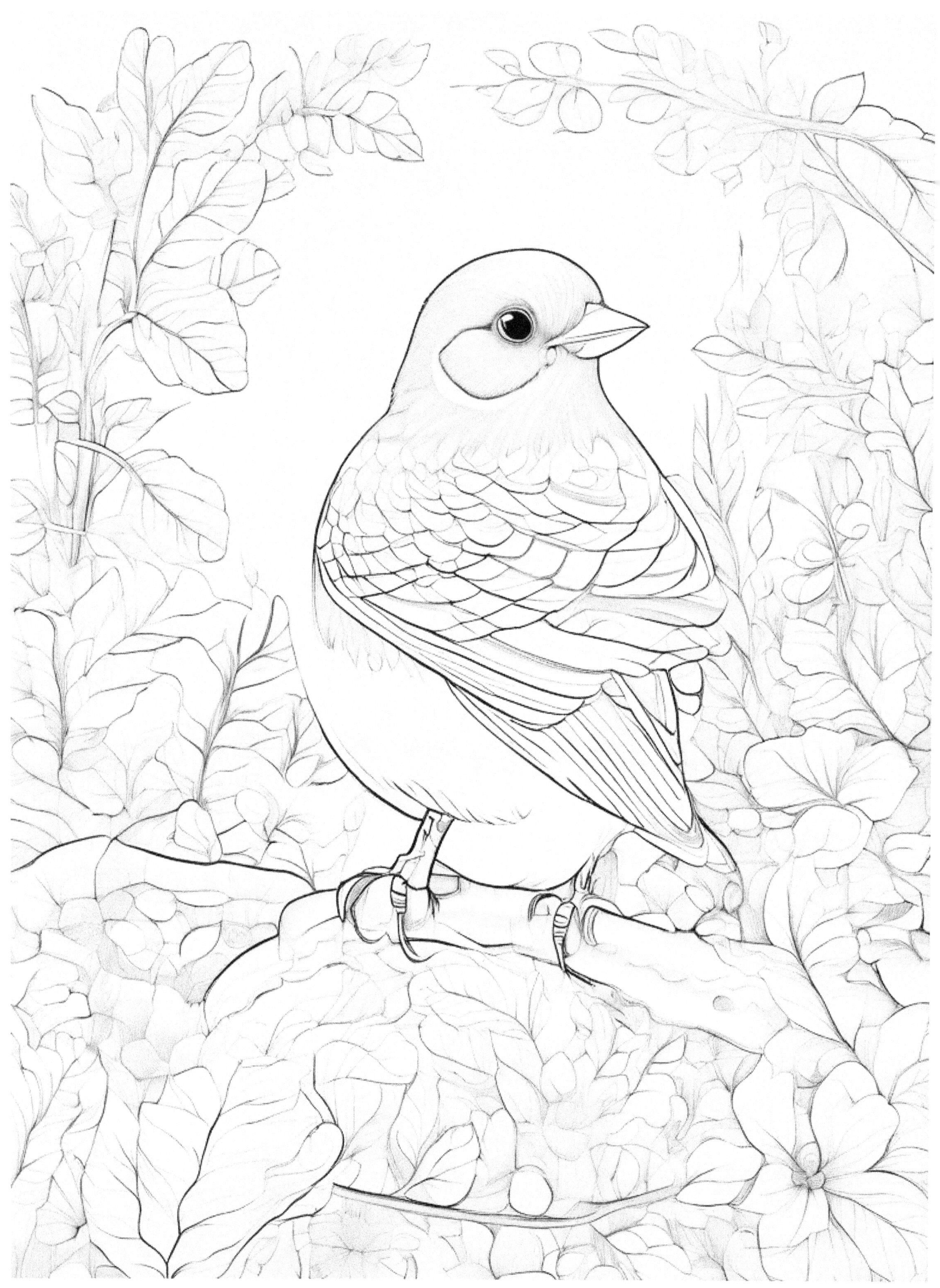

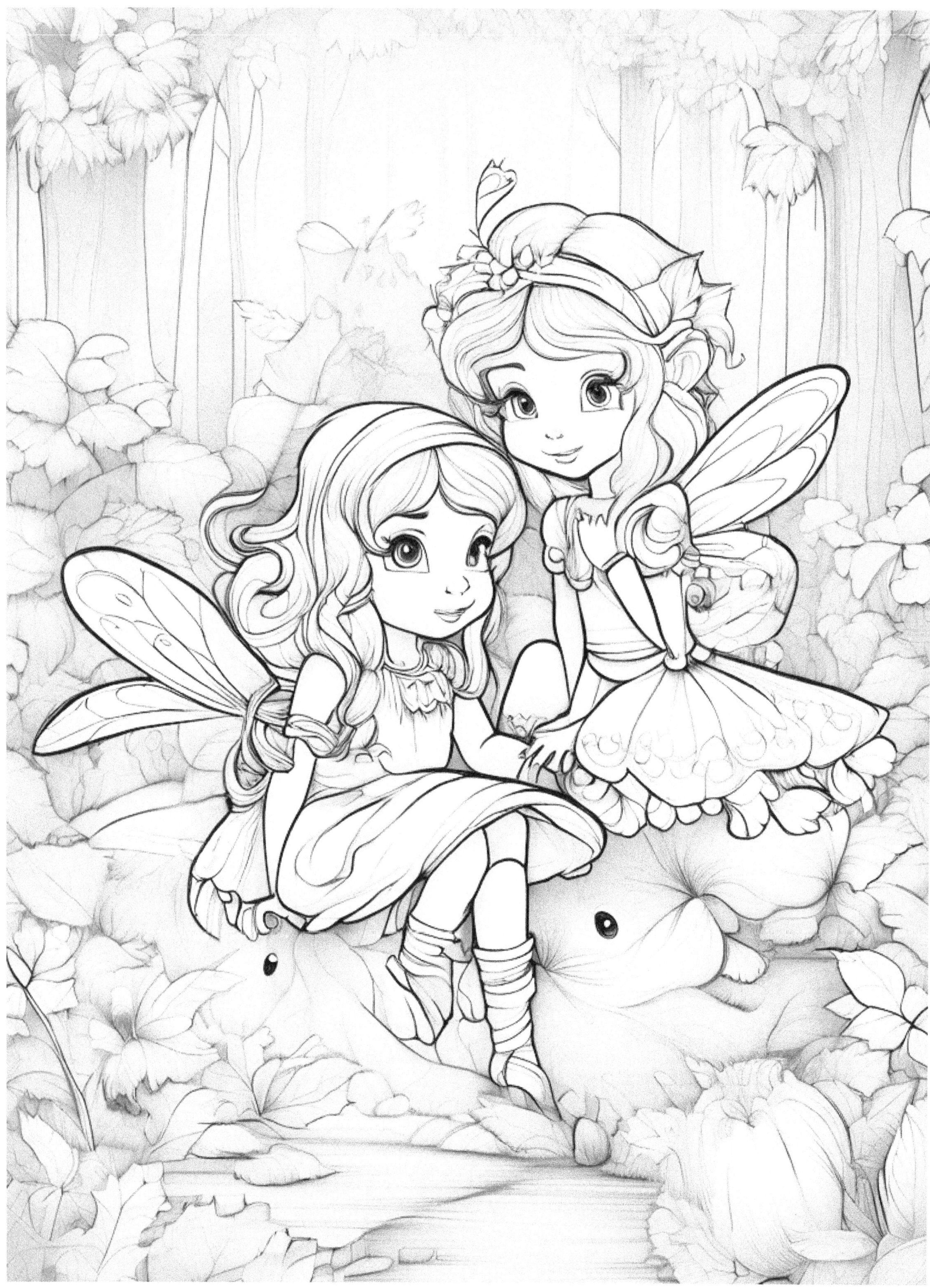

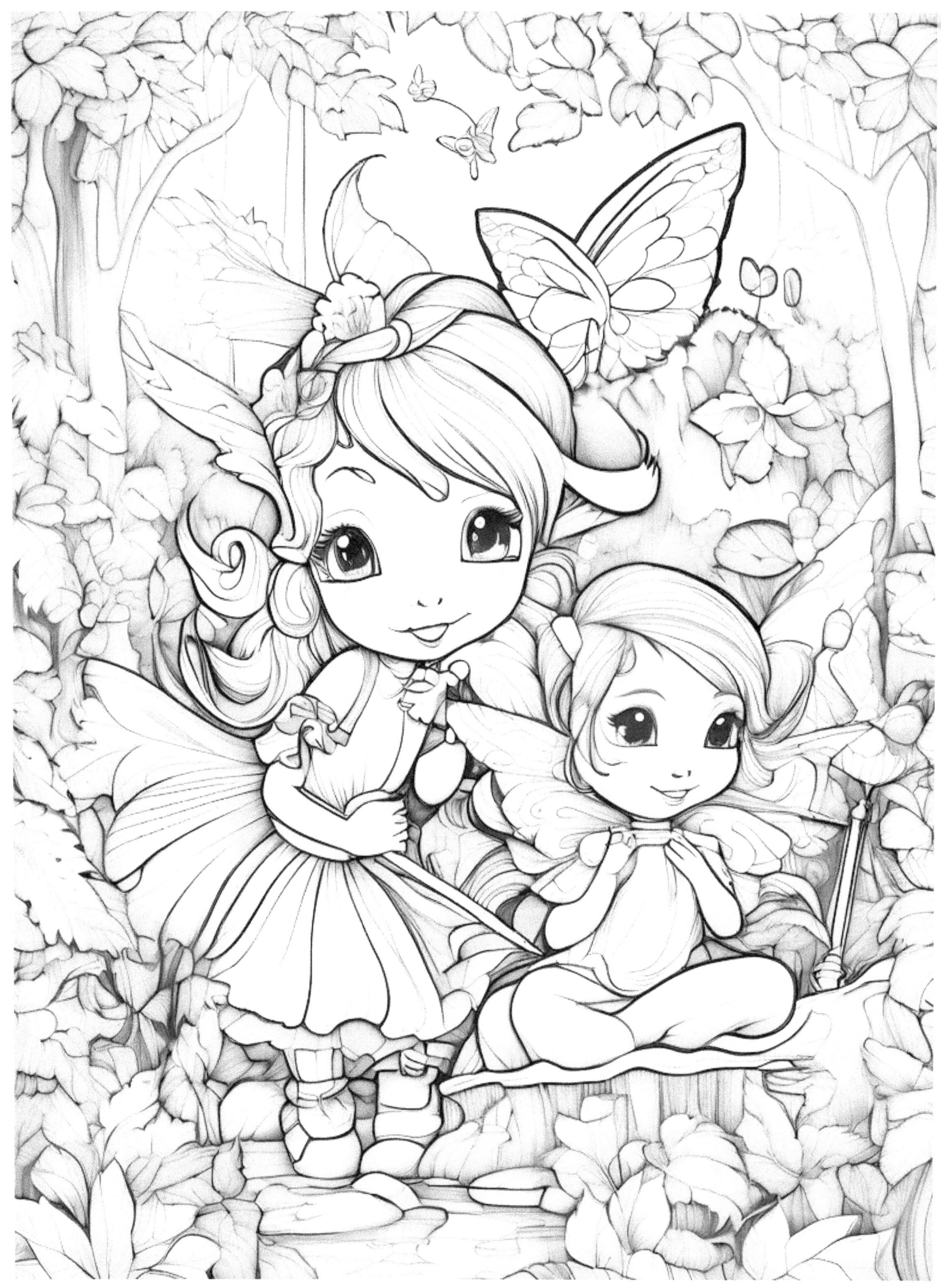

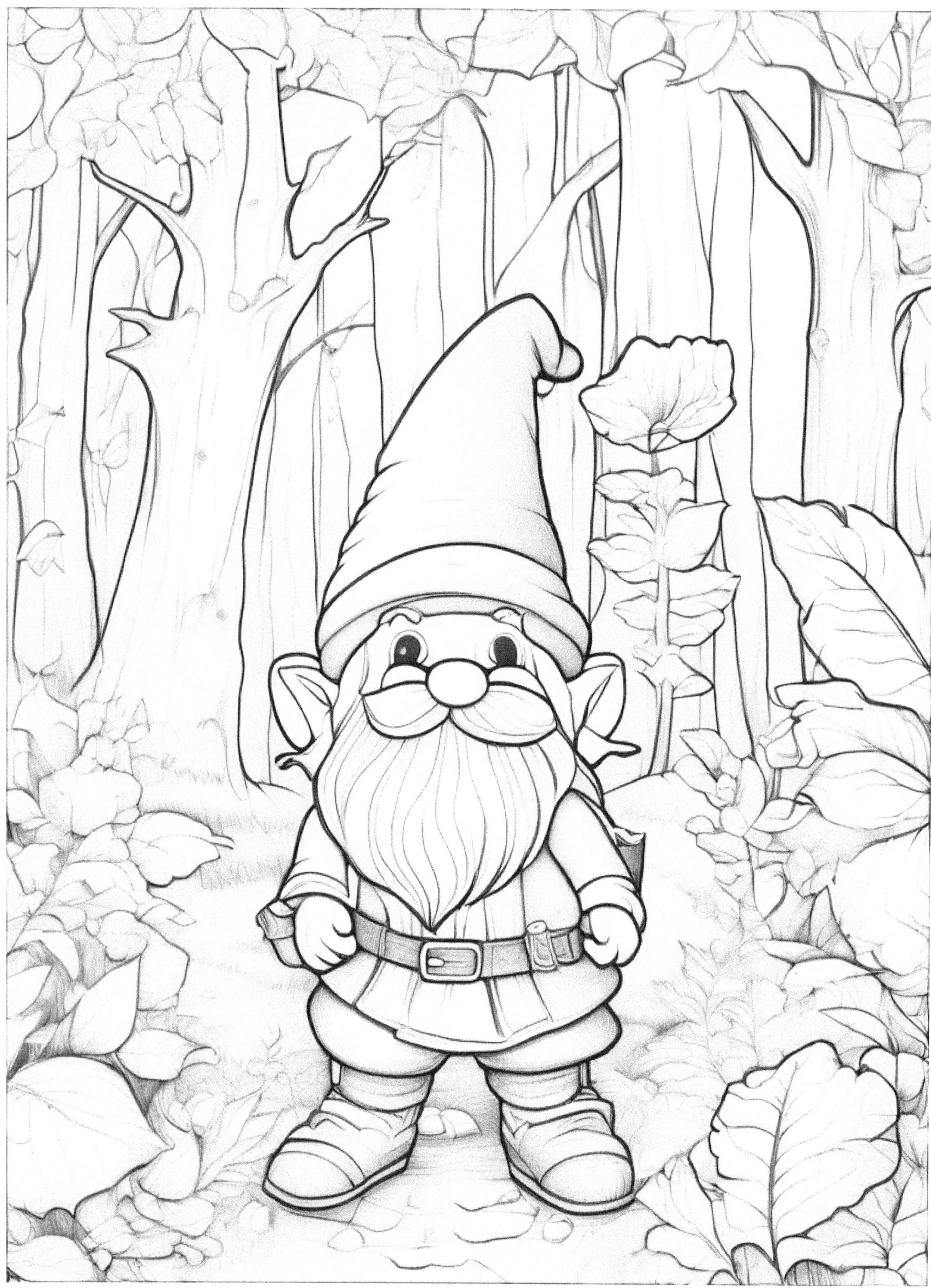

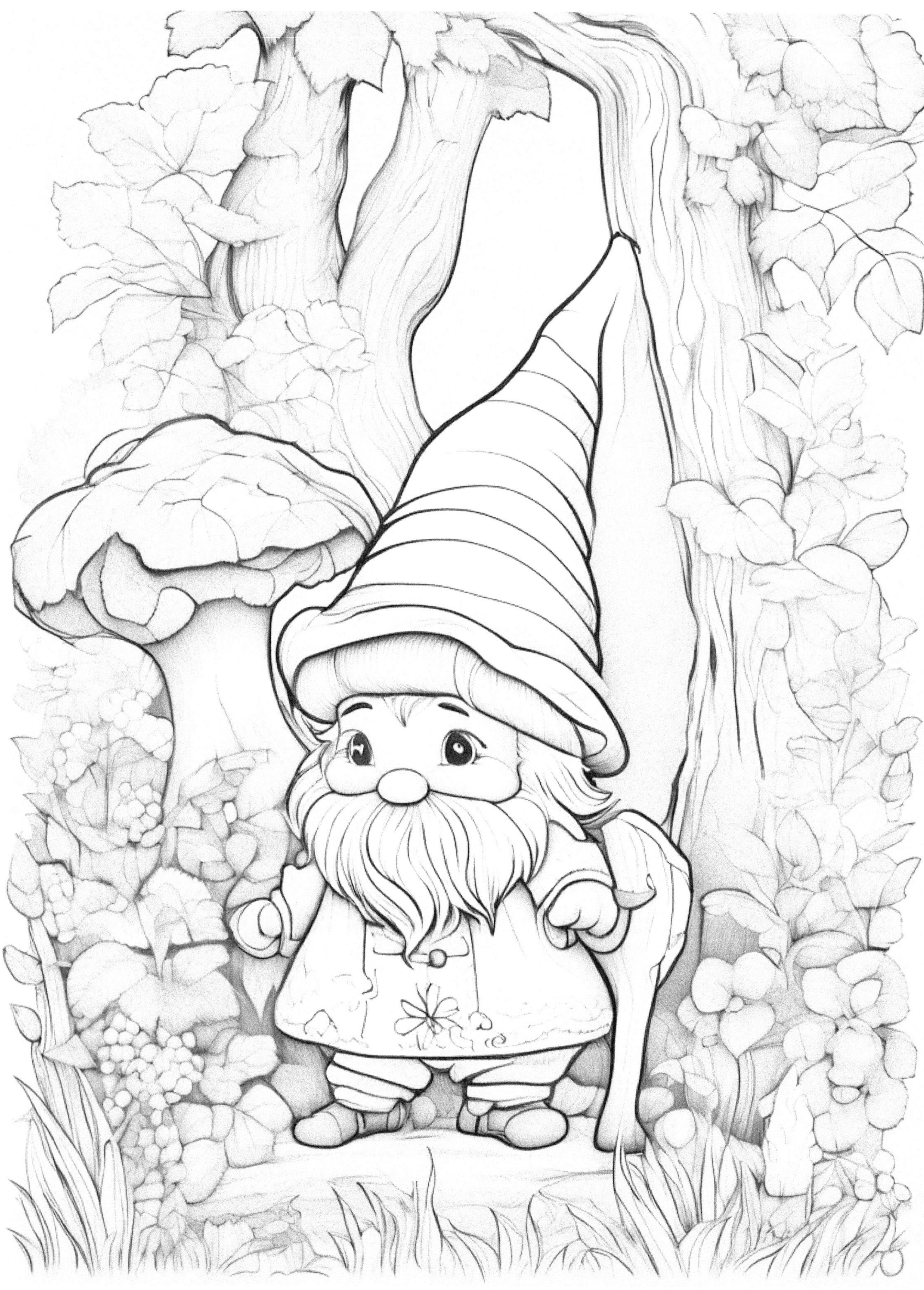

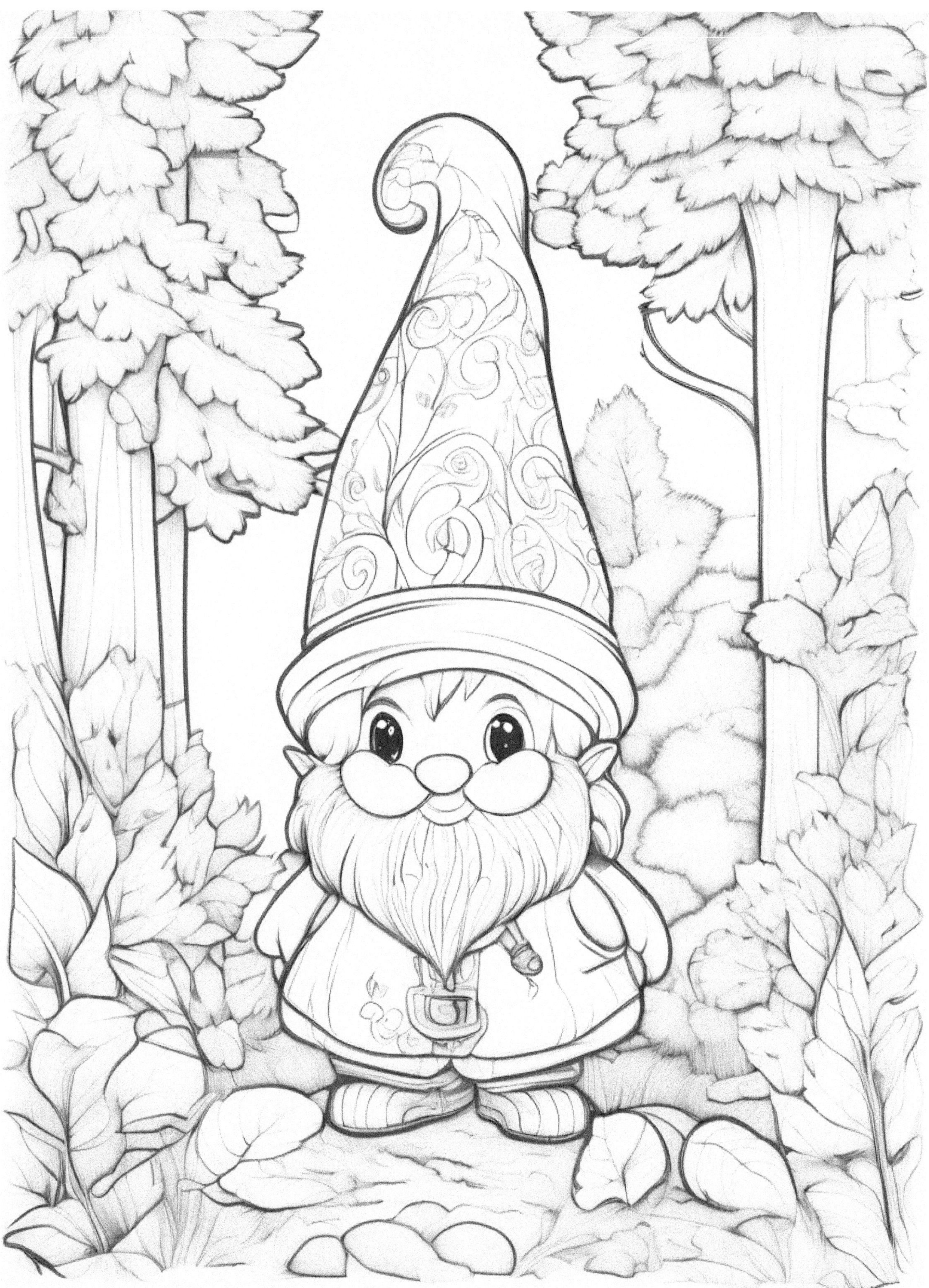

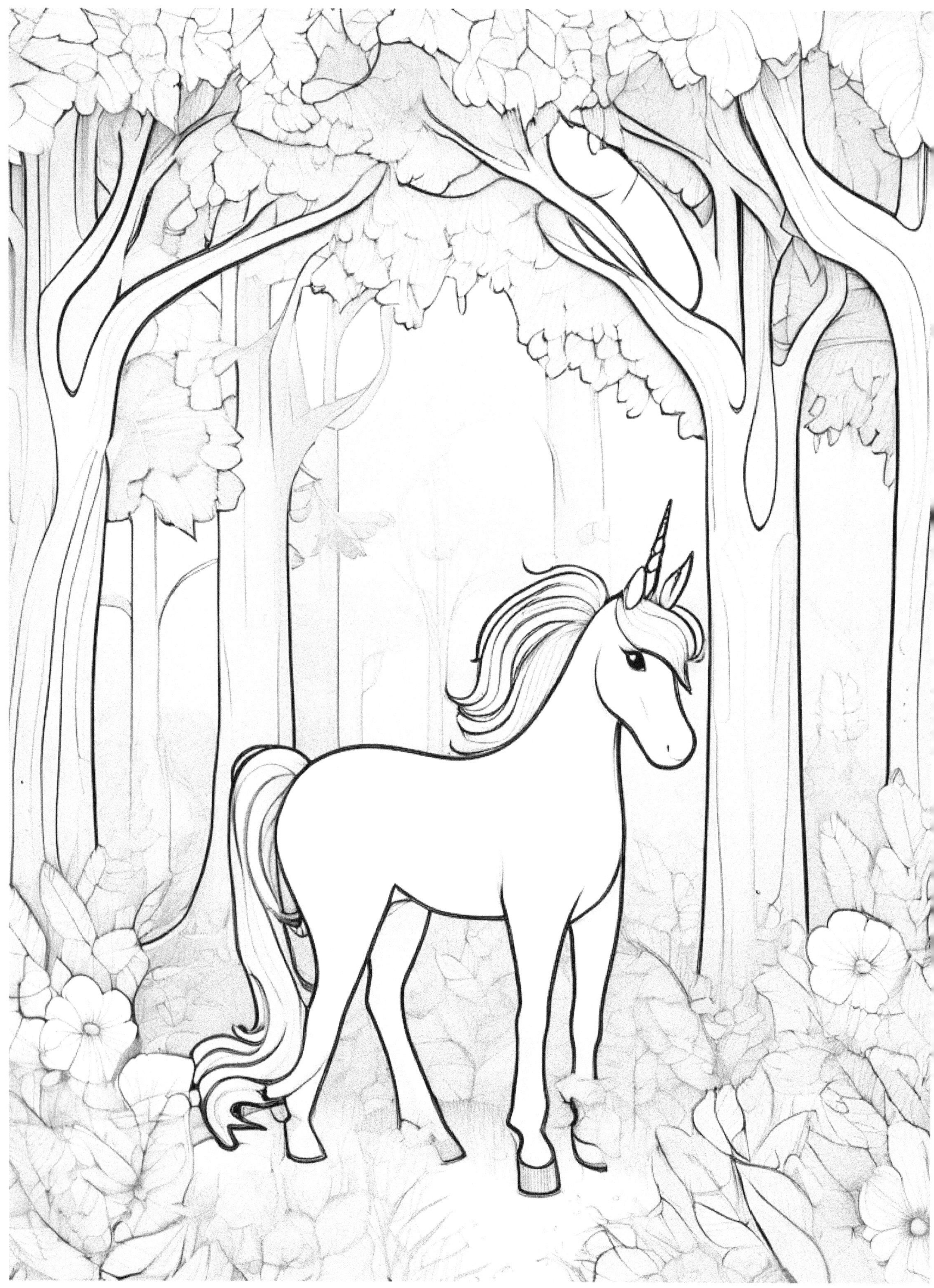

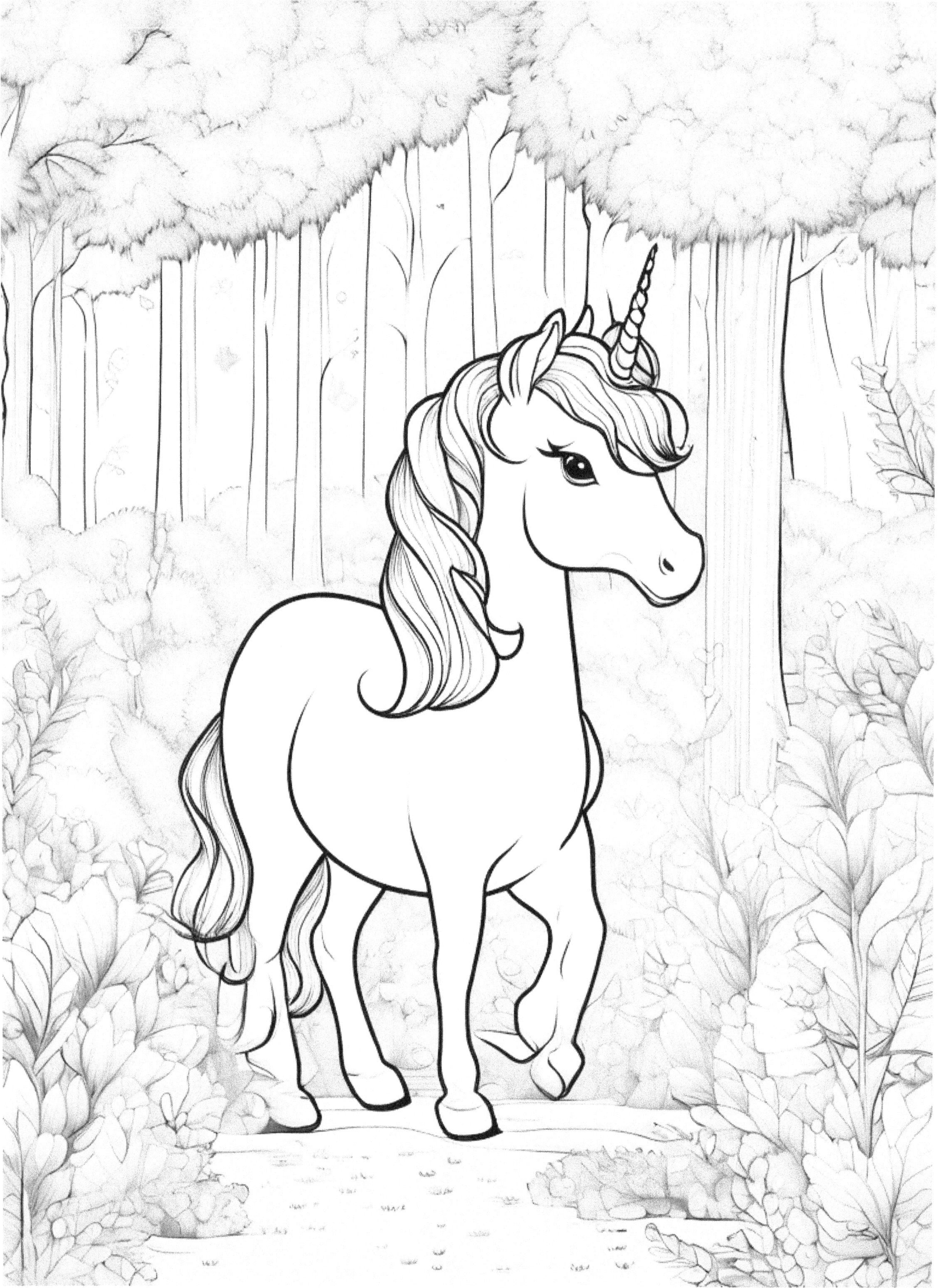

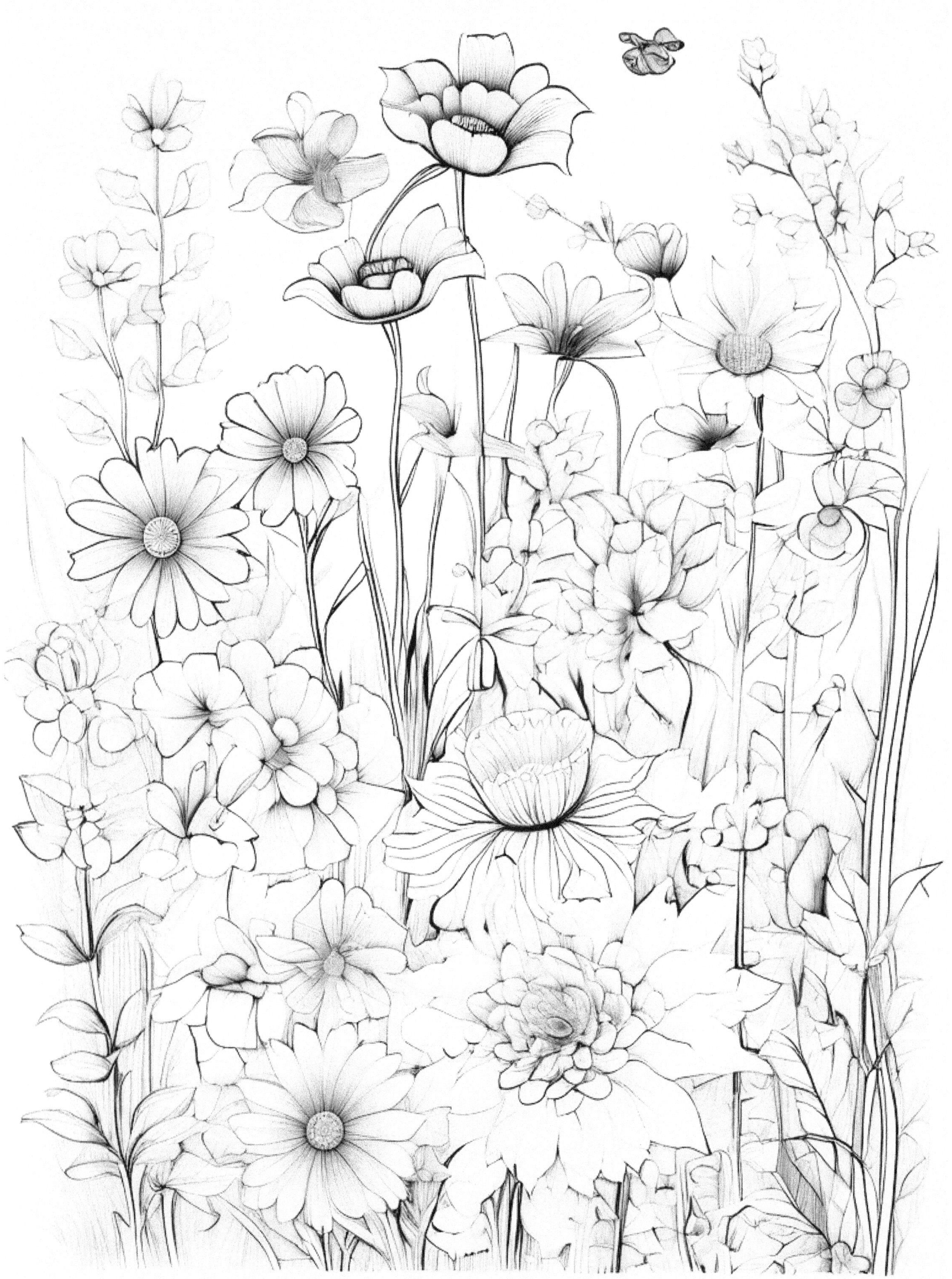

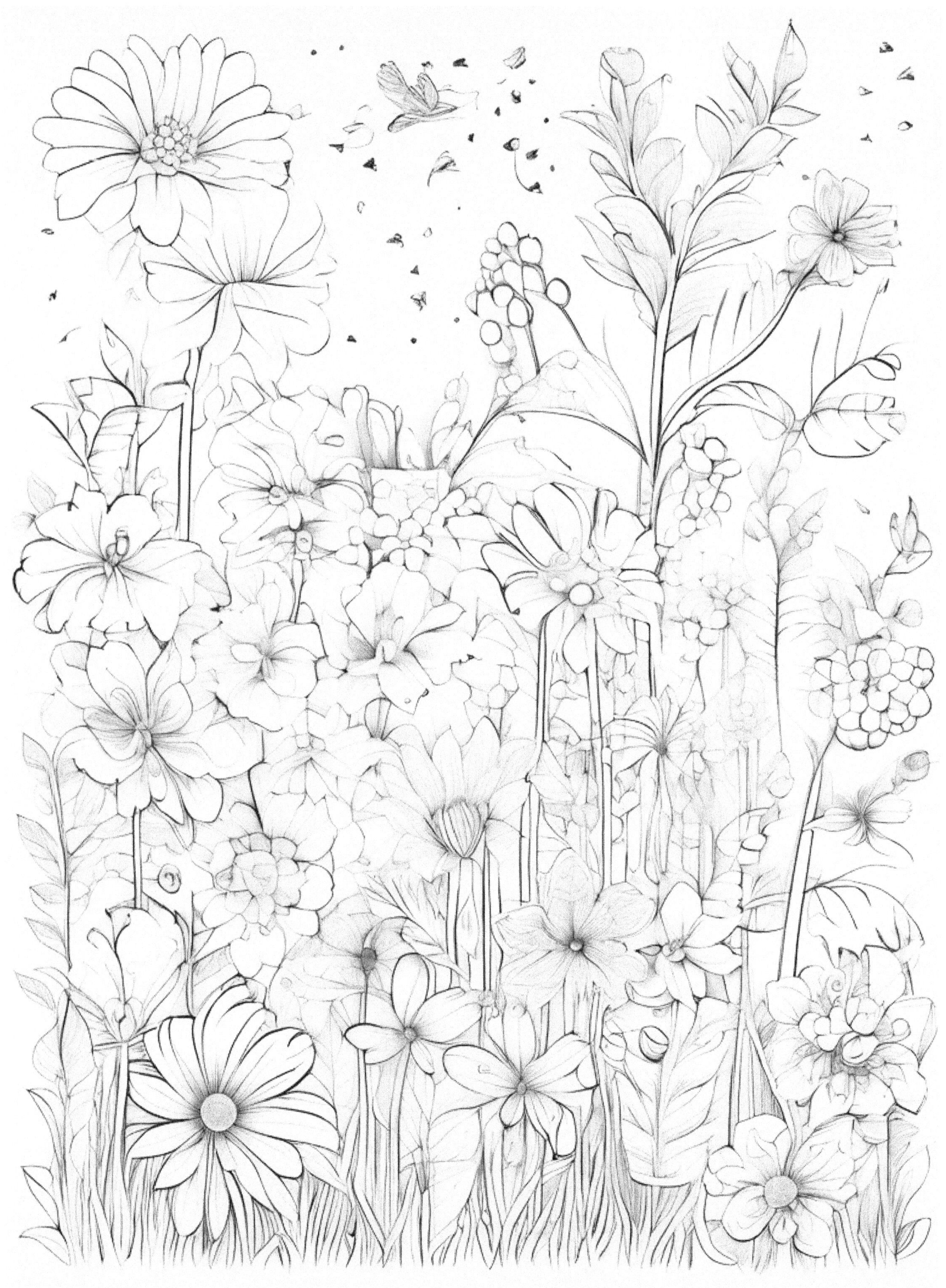

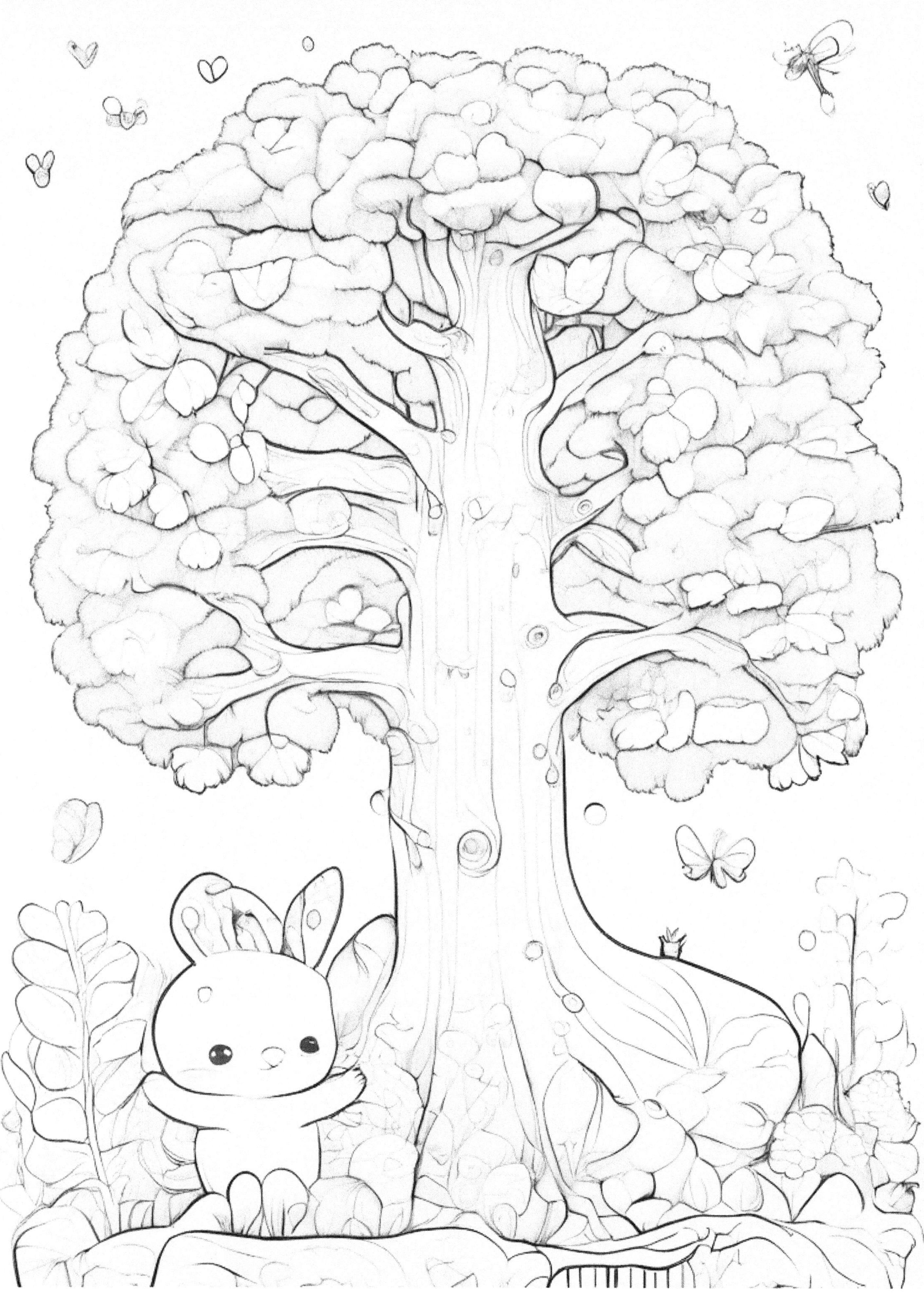

For your creativity

For your creativity

For your creativity

For your creativity

For your creativity

For your creativity

Special Thanks:

"To our dear readers who have reached the end of this colorful journey,
We sincerely thank you for sharing this magical moment with us. We hope the
pages of this book have brought you joy and inspiration. Thank you for
allowing the magic of colors to brighten your world.
With warmth,

— Tainá Oishi"